Financial Life Cycle Mathematics

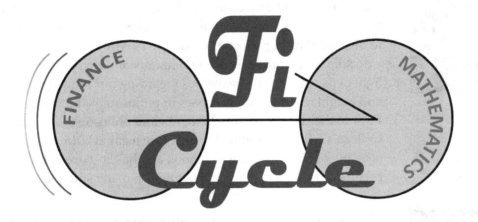

Student Workbook

Jack Marley-Payne, Philip Dituri, Andrew Davidson

ABOUT THE AUTHORS

Jack Marley-Payne researches issues in education, finance and mathematics, and creates materials for teaching and understanding these topics. Jack grew up in the UK and moved to the US in order to obtain a PhD in philosophy from MIT. While there, he completed a doctoral dissertation focused on understanding knowledge in the light of psychological discoveries regarding our limited rationality, and taught undergraduate classes in philosophy and mathematics. Prior to this, he studied mathematics and philosophy at Exeter College, Oxford. Jack joined the FiCycle team in 2015, before it had been piloted in a single high school, and has been excited to see it become a thriving program, benefiting so many students.

Philip Dituri, Ph.D., is a mathematics educator and consultant. He served as a Visiting Professor at Fordham University, and was a teacher, mathematics instructional coach, and chairperson of the mathematics department at New Design High School in Manhattan. While working in public school, he was a three-time Math for America Master Teacher and a Big Apple Award finalist. Phil has a B.A. in Mathematics from NYU and a Ph.D. in Mathematics Education from Columbia University. His research interests include proof and reasoning, problem solving, collaborative learning, remote learning, and personal finance.

Andrew Davidson is a financial innovator and leader in the development of financial research and analytics, as well as the founder of FiCycle. He is president of Andrew Davidson & Co., Inc., a New York firm specializing in the application of analytical tools to investment management, which he founded in 1992. Andrew was instrumental in the creation of the Freddie Mac and Fannie Mae risk-sharing transactions, allowing them to attract private capital to bear credit risk, even as they remain in government conservatorship. Andrew is also active in other dimensions of GSE reform and has testified before the Senate Banking Committee on multiple occasions.

Acknowledgements: A great many wonderful people offered their time and wisdom to provide improvements to this book. Special thanks go to Alysia DaSilva, Bjorn Flesaker, Finn Kreidler, Gio Donovan, Jacob Katzman, Karie Parker Davidson, Karina Minchuk, Lauren Davidson, Paul Gray, Photo Anagnostopoulos, and Rose Davidson.

Table of Contents

How to use this Workbook 6

Financial Research Materials 7

Unit 2: Earning Interest

INTRODUCTORY MATERIAL.. 8

TOPIC 1: INTRODUCTION TO EARNING INTEREST 9

    Transferring Money through Time: Borrowing and Investing 11

    Value and Time 13

    Unit 2 Topic 1 Check for Understanding 15

TOPIC 2: MATHEMATICS OF INTEREST 17

    Simple Interest 19

    Compound Interest 21

    Comparing Simple and Compound Interest 24

    Unit 2 Topic 2 Check for Understanding 28

TOPIC 3: THE COMPOUND INTEREST FORMULA 32

    Comparing Simple and Compound Interest (within a year)............... 36

    Euler's Number 39

    Continuous Compounding 41

    Comparing Varieties of Compounding 43

    Unit 2 Topic 3 Check for Understanding 44

TOPIC 4: THE RULE OF 72 – DOUBLE YOUR MONEY 49

    Simple to Continuous Compounding 53

    Rule of 72 55

    Converting other kinds of Compounding (Extension)...................... 60

    Unit 2 Topic 4 Check for Understanding 62

TOPIC 5: PRESENT VALUE 65

    Where does the discounting rate come from? 66

    Applying the Rule of 72 68

    Unit 2 Topic 5 Check for Understanding 69

TOPIC 6: EARNING INTEREST IN THE FINANCIAL LIFE CYCLE............. 72

    Introducing the Financial Life Cycle 72

    Unpacking the Financial Life Cycle... 75

4

Unit 3: Regular Payments

How to use this Workbook

This workbook is the primary document you will use to learn about the material in unit 1 of FiCycle. It provides explanations of all the vocabulary and ideas you need to know, along with examples and exercises to help you cement your understanding.

You can read through the document page by page, doing the questions as you go, or use it as your teacher instructs.

Here are the icons to look out for throughout the document:

 Vocabulary: This introduces a new piece of vocabulary, either financial or mathematical, along with a definition of the term.

 Question: This is a question you must answer. When you see this icon, it means you must do something. It's important you don't skip it!

 Reflection Question: This is also a question that you need to answer. This time, though, it is an invitation to reflect, and does not have a single correct answer. You should feel free to write what comes to mind without worrying about getting it wrong.

 Math Check: This is a worksheet to check you have the math skills you will need for the next section. Work through the questions to check and practice your skills. If you are not comfortable completing the sheet, ask your teacher for additional help.

 Spreadsheet: This icon means that there is an activity you must complete on a separate spreadsheet document. There will be information on the document you need to access and instructions on what to do.

 Extension: This is a question or activity you can do to deepen your knowledge of the material. It is an optional part of the course that you may choose to skip past if your teacher allows it.

 Connection to the Life Cycle: This indicates a relationship between the topic you're working on and the overarching theme of the financial life cycle.

Financial Research Materials

In this course, you will have to research real financial products. This is practice for the real world where you don't just have to understand the financial products, you also have to know how to find the best deal.

Here is a list of some of the sites that will help you.

Financial Comparison Sites:

These sites allow you to compare various financial products meeting certain criteria – e.g. credit card with no annual fee. Comparison sites are a convenient way to shop around for the best deal without having to go through a large number of different websites by yourself. Some of the most common are:

https://www.nerdwallet.com/
https://www.creditkarma.com/
https://www.creditcards.com/

Be careful though, since these sites have sponsors, whose products they may promote. Make sure you check the details for yourself on any product you consider – don't just take the site's word for it when it says a product is your best option. More information on this can be found in the following article:

http://business.time.com/2012/08/10/do-credit-card-comparison-sites-work-as-promised/

Specialty Sites:

https://www.zillow.com/
>   This site provides information on homes, both to rent and to buy
>   You can search by area, price, size etc.

https://www.salaryexpert.com/salary/
>   This site provides information on the salary of various jobs

https://www.numbeo.com/
>   This site provides information on cost of living in locations around the world
>   It provides specific information on the cost of food, healthcare, and transit by location

As websites change over time, up to date links will be provided on the FiCycle website.

UNIT 2: EARNING INTEREST

INTRODUCTORY MATERIAL

Looking Ahead

Over a financial life cycle, the income you receive at a given time will not always match what you need to consume, you can transfer money either forward or backward so you can consume it when you need it. You transfer money forward by investing and transfer it backwards by borrowing. Typically, you will be paid to transfer money forward, and must pay to transfer it backward. Learning about investment strategy is a central part of the financial life cycle, and this requires understanding exponents and logs.

After completing this unit, you will be able to:

- Understand concepts related to earning interest
- Calculate simple interest
- Understand compounding
- Calculate compound interest
- Calculate continuously compounded interest
- Move between simple interest and continuously compounded interest
- Use the rule of 72
- Calculate present value using discounting
- Know the cost and benefits of the financial instruments used for borrowing and investing
- Understand the importance of credit scores
- Use interest calculations to create financial statements
- Apply exponents and logarithms to financial material

TOPIC 1: INTRODUCTION TO EARNING INTEREST

You are just about to leave for school when a strange raggedy man shows up on your doorstep. He asks to use your bathroom and in return offers you a gift.

He is a time traveler and will give you something he took from the past. You have two options:

1. A set of solid gold jewel-encrusted eggs (known as 'Fabergé eggs') that he stole from Russian royalty during the 1917 revolution.
2. The rights to a bank account with Banca Monte dei Paschi di Siena, the world's oldest surviving bank, that he opened in 1472 when the bank was founded and that he hasn't touched since.

1. Which will you choose?

A set of Faberge Eggs – image source *http://www.saint-petersburg.com/famous-people/peter-carl-faberge/*

Some more information:
- The combined value of the eggs is over $300 million
- The time-traveler deposited a single dollar in the bank account when he opened it and has made no further deposits or withdrawals for 545 years.

2. Does this affect your choice?

Monte dei Paschi di Siena Headquarter's Main Entrance. Image source: *https://en.wikipedia.org/wiki/Banca_Monte_dei_Paschi_di_Siena*

Even more information:

Now you learn that due to a special introductory offer, this bank account was guaranteed 5% interest rate for as long as it remained open.

- Because of this, the value today after 545 years is over $350 *billion*.

Reminder on units:

- A **million** is a thousand times a thousand, so $1 million = $1,000,000
- A **billion** is a thousand times a million, so $1 billion = $1,000,000,000
- A **trillion** is a thousand times a billion, so $1 trillion = $1,000,000,000,000

If you want more practice dealing with these large units, look at our supplemental worksheet 'Unit 2 Topic 1 Math Sheet Millions Billions Trillions'

3. Did you make the right choice?

The reason the value of the bank account is so high is due to something called **compound interest**, which is the topic of this unit.

Transferring Money through Time: Borrowing and Investing

Over a financial life cycle, the income you receive at a given time will not always match what you need to consume; you can transfer money either forward or backward so you can consume it when you need it.

Investing is when you transfer money forward *to* your future self.

Borrowing is when you transfer money backwards *from* your future self.
- Typically, you will be paid to transfer money forward, and must pay to transfer it backward.

An **investment** is money transferred to the future from the present by means of a financial product.
- When people have money that is not needed for immediate expenses, they may choose to invest it (this extra money is known as a **surplus**).
- They transfer their **surplus** to someone who needs cash to meet immediate needs – either a bank or another financial company, a government, or an individual.
- When investing, one expects to receive one's money back at a later date and to be paid for the service in the form of receiving money beyond that which was originally invested.
- Common reasons to invest include saving money for retirement, for a down payment on a house, for a child's education.
- Typically, the purpose of investing is to help one meet future financial goals.

A **loan** is money transferred to the present from the future by means of a financial product.
- A **loan** is a financial instrument that lets you *borrow* money from your future self.
  - In other words: A loan is a tool that allows you to spend your future income in the present.
- Sometimes you do not have money available to meet a current financial need – either to purchase an asset or cover expenses.
- Through a loan you may acquire money from a company, a bank, or an individual to meet such needs.
- You will have to return the money as well as pay the lender for the service.
- Common reasons to borrow include paying for education, paying for a house, and paying for a car.

Because of the workings of loans and investments, the value of money invested or borrowed changes over time.

12

- Money increases in value if saved for the future. For example, you loan your money to a person or institution and they pay you for the use of your money.

Interest is the additional value you pay or receive over time when you borrow or invest.

We use specific terminology for interest when borrowing and investing:
- When you invest, you **earn** interest – earning interest is a form of income.
- When you borrow, your loan **accrues** interest – accruing interest is a form of expense

The initial amount of money deposited or invested is known as the **principal**.

[*Word bank*: more; less; loan; investment; future; earn; pay; surplus; past; deficiency; loan; investing; borrowing]

4. If you now possess money that you don't need it's called a _Surplus_. You can transfer this money to the future by _investing_

5. You borrow money if you need to spend _future_ income now.

6. In order to borrow money, you must take out a _loan_.

7. When you invest, you generally receive _More_ money than you put in, but you receive it at a later date.

8. If you borrow money, you will _pay_ interest.

9. If you invest, you will _earn_ interest.

10. Decide whether each of the following financial goals will likely be met by investing, borrowing, or a bit of both. Explain your answer.
    a. Having money available when you retire _investing_
    b. Starting up a new business _borrowing_
    c. c) Paying college fees _borrowing / investing_
    d. d) Providing an inheritance for your children. _investing_

11. Provide your own example of a financial goal that should be met through investing – explain your answer.

12. Provide your own example of a financial goal that should be met through borrowing – explain your answer.

Value and Time

This unit will look at the effects of interest and its role in the financial life cycle. To do this, we need thee key concepts: (1) future value; (2) present value; (3) interest rate.

 Future value (FV) is the value a given sum of money will be worth at a certain point in the future.

Example: You invest $1000 for 3 years – the value of your investment after 3 years is its **future value.**

Present value (PV) is the *current value* of a given sum of money that will be received at some point in the future.

Example: Your friend agrees to pay you $80 in six months' time if you pay her $50 now – the **present value** of the loan is $50.

 13. You invest $200 in a savings account and after 5 years the account balance is $230.

    a. What is the present value of your investment?

    b. What is the future value of your investment?

14. You invest $35 in your cousin's startup, and after 5 years the startup has tripled in value.

    a. What is the present value of your investment?

    b. What is the future value of your investment?

 Interest rate (r) is the percentage of money you earn or pay for investing or borrowing each year.

- The interest you earn or pay is proportional to the amount of money you invest: you earn interest as a *percentage* of the original amount. This percentage value is called the **interest rate**.
- *Notation*: We will express an interest rate where you earn five percent of the amount invested as "5%".

Example: You invest $100 with an interest rate of 3%. This means that the interest you earn is 3% of $100: $3.

 15. You borrow $75 with a 60% interest rate – what is the interest on your loan?

A note on time: The interest rate is an **annual** measure – you receive the interest after a year of investing (or borrowing.)

Example: Ava invests $1000 in a savings account for a year. The interest rate is 1% Let's look at what happens after a year.

- After a year, Ava will be paid her interest, which is the interest rate multiplied by the present value: 1000·0.01=10
- So after a year, Ava will have $1010
- This means that the future value of the investment is $1010 – we write FV=1010.
- Conversely, the present value of the investment is $1000 – we write PV=1000

16. Carlos borrows $250. The interest rate is 30%. How much will Carlos owe after a year has passed?

Next Question: What happens if you invest or borrow over more than one year?
- To answer this, we need to look at the *mathematics of interest* in the next section.

Unit 2 Topic 1 Check for Understanding

Section 1. Complete the following definitions, using the word bank below:

[Word Bank: time-value-of-money, accrue, backward, earn, future-value, lend, forward, borrow, interest, principal, present-value, loan]

1. Interest is earned when you transfer consumption _forward_ in time.

2. Investments _earn_ interest, while loans _accrue_ interest.

3. If you want to know how much your investment will be worth after a certain time, you are interested in its _future-value_.

4. An investment's _present-value_ is how much it's worth now.

5. Investments are transactions in which you _lend_ excess income to other institutions.

6. The price you pay to use borrowed money is called _interest_.

7. The fundamental principle of the _time value of money_ is that dollars received today are more valuable than dollars promised in the future.

8. If you want to use future income for present expenses you need a _loan_.

Section 2. Circle all correct answer(s). There might be more than one correct answer:

9. People transfer money forward in time because:
   a. The government makes them
   b. They want to consume more than they will earn in the future
   c. They don't currently want to buy anything
   d. They like to describe themselves as an investor to their crush

10. If you invest with a 5% interest rate, *when* you will get the 5% interest?
    a. After you ask for it enough times
    b. When you truly need it
    c. After you do 1000 push-ups
    d. After a year

11. Which of the following are good reasons to borrow money?
    a. You think we're near the end of days, so you will never have to pay it back
    ⓑ So you can buy an asset that will reduce expenses in the long run
    ⓒ To pay for courses to earn a college degree that will increase your income
    d. Your friends will be impressed if you have a lot of cash in your wallet

Section 3. Show all work.

12. Elise borrows $1000. The interest rate is 15%.
    a. How much interest will accrue in one year?

    $(1000)(.15) = 150$ dollars

    b. How much money will Elise owe in one year?

    1150 dollars

13. Ronald borrows $1,000,000 from his father. Since they are family, his father gives him an amazingly low interest rate of 0.3%.
    a. How much interest will Ronald accrue in one year?

    $(1000,000)(.003) = 3000$ dollars

    b. How much money will Ronald owe in one year?

    $1,003,000$ dollars

14. Harry borrows $1,234 from Dudley with an interest rate of 5.6%.
    a. How much interest will Harry accrue in one year?

    $(1234)(.056) = 69.104$ dollars

    b. How much money will Harry owe in one year?

    1303.101 dollars

TOPIC 2: MATHEMATICS OF INTEREST

Math Check 1: Exponents

To understand the material in this topic, you must be comfortable with exponents – test your knowledge with the following questions:
- *Note*: You also need to be comfortable with fractions to answer these questions. If you need help with this, ask your teacher.

Section 1. Multiplying Powers

Example: $x^4 \cdot x^3 = x$
General Rule: $a^m \cdot a^n = a^{m+n}$

1. $z^2 * z^7 = 2^9$

2. $3xy^3 \cdot 6x^4y^8 = 18x^5y^{11}$

Section 2. Dividing Powers

Example: $\frac{x^7}{x^2} = x^5$
General Rule: $\frac{a^m}{a^n} = a^{m-n}$

3. $\frac{y^{16}}{y^9} = y^7$

4. $\frac{q^3r^8}{qr^2} = q^2r^6$

Section 3. Raising a Power to a Power

Example: $\left(x^8\right)^3 = x^{24}$
General Rule: $(a^m)^n = a^{m*n}$

5. $\left(x^4\right)^{12} = x^{48}$

6. $\left(x^6\right)^4 5y^7 = x^{24}5y^7$

18

Section 4. Distribution of powers

Example: $(xy)^4 = x^4y^4$

General Rule: $(ab)^n = a^nb^n$

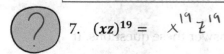

7. $(xz)^{19} = x^{19}z^{19}$

8. $(5x^6y^3)^2 = 25x^{12}y^6$

Section 5. Zero Exponents

General Rule: $a^0 = 1$

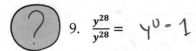

9. $\frac{y^{28}}{y^{28}} = y^0 = 1$

10. $7x^2z^0 \cdot 3x = 21x^3$

Simple Interest

It is important that we can calculate the future value of an investment, given information about principal and interest rate.

- There are two different ways of earning interest: (1) **simple interest** and (2) **compound interest**.

We'll start by looking at **simple interest**.

Simple interest over a year: Over one year, with interest rate r, you earn r of your deposit.
- For example, if r = 5%, you would earn 5% of the amount you deposited. Thus, any amount you deposit now will be worth an additional 5% in the future.

Example: You invest $1000 with interest rate of 8%, with **simple interest**. How much will you have after a year?
- After a year you will receive $1000 \cdot r = 1000 \cdot 0.08 = 80$ in interest.
- Since you still have your initial $1000, you will have $1080 in total.

11. Identify the values of the following variables in this example.
    a. Future Value: FV=_____
    b. Present value: PV=_____
    c. Interest rate: r=_____

In general, after one year, the value of your investment is the sum of the initial value (PV) and that initial value multiplied by the interest rate (r). To put it symbolically:

- $FV = PV + r \bullet PV = PV \bullet (1 + r)$ [We factor out PV to simplify]

Simple interest over multiple years: If you earn interest on your deposit over multiple years, you will earn r of your deposit multiple times.

Example: You earn 8% interest on $1000 each year for 3 years; you end up with your initial $1000, along with three sets of 8% of $1000
- That is, you'll have $1000 + 1000 \bullet 0.08 \bullet 3 = 1000(1 + 0.08 \bullet 3)$; which is $1240.

12. You invest $245 with interest rate 14.6%. How much will you have after earning simple interest for 2 years?

20

We can see a general pattern here: if you invest with simple interest for a certain number of years, you end up with that number of sets of the rate multiplied by the principal (along with the principal itself).

- Symbolically, if you invest for t years, you will end up with $PV + PV \cdot r \cdot t$; this gives us the **simple interest formula**:

Simple Interest Formula: $FV = PV \bullet (1 + rt)$

Formula Key:
FV = Future Value
PV = Present Value
r = Rate
t = Number of years

---

13. You invest $950 for 12 years with a simple interest rate of 5.3%. How much will you end up with? Use the simple interest formula (above), and state what values you assigned to each variable.

14. You invest $11 for 48 years with a simple interest rate of 9%. How much will you end up with? Use the simple interest formula, and state what values you assigned to each variable.

15. You invest $30,000 for 6 years with a simple interest rate of 15%. How much will you end up with? Use the simple interest formula, and state what values you assigned to each variable.

Compound Interest

Usually if you invest over multiple years, you will earn *interest on your interest*, this is known as **compounding**.

- Each year you earn r of the amount you have at the end of the previous year (including both our principal *and* your interest from the past year)

Example: You invest $50 for two years with compound interest at a rate of 10%.
- In the first year, you earn 10% of $50 so you have $55 at the end of the year.
- In the second year you earn, 10% of $55 so you end up with $55 + 0.1 \cdot 55 = 60.5$

16. How much will you earn if you invest $125,000 for two years, with compound interest rate of 4%?

Now let's look at things symbolically, using *PV* for present value, *FV* for future value, *r* for interest rate, and *t* for time. In the table below we will start with the present value of a loan and calculate interest year over year to see how compound interest works.

Formula	Explanation
PV	The Present Value of your investment.
$PV + PV \bullet r$ $PV \bullet (1 + r)$	This is the value of your investment after one year. We simplify by factoring out PV.
$PV \bullet (1 + r) \bullet r$	This is the interest you earn after the second year – we take the total at the end of one year and multiply by r.
$PV \bullet (1 + r) + PV \bullet (1 + r) \bullet r$ $PV \bullet (1 + r) \bullet (1 + r)$ $PV \bullet (1 + r)^2$	This is the total value of your investment after two years. We simplify by factoring out PV and $(1+r)$. We simplify using the laws of exponents.
$PV \bullet (1 + r)^n$	Suppose after n years this is the value of the investment We want to know its value after another year (n+1 years).

$\begin{array}{c} PV \bullet (1+r)^n + PV \bullet (1+r)^n \cdot (1 \\ +r) \\ PV \bullet (1+r)^n(1+r) \\ PV \bullet (1+r)^{n+1} \end{array}$	We sum the initial amount with that amount multiplied by r. We factor out $PV \bullet (1+r)^n$. We simplify using the laws of exponents.

This tells us that in general, when you earn compound interest for t years, the following equation holds:

Simple Compounding Interest Formula: $FV = PV \bullet (1+r)^t$

Formula Key:

FV = Future Value

PV = Present Value

r = Rate

t = Number of years

Note: This is a special instance of the **compound interest formula** that we will discuss in topic 2.

Example: Suppose you invest $1000 for 3 years at a rate of 8%, then: $FV = 1000 \bullet (1.08)^3 = 1259.71$

- We calculated above that if you earned **simple interest** of $1000 at 8% for three years, you would have had $1240, so earning interest on your interest got you an additional $19.71!

17. You invest $450 for 30 years with compound interest at rate of 9.7%. What is the future value of your investment?

18. You take out a bad loan for $900 with an interest rate of 28%. How much do you owe after 15 years if you don't make any payments?

19. Rose has access to an account that earns 5% interest every year. She reasons that if she deposits $100 , she will make $10 after two years and have a total of $110. Is she correct? Explain.

Note: In almost all real-world investments, interest over multiple years is compounded, not simple. **Unless otherwise stated, assume interest is compounded in all examples and problems in this book.**

Spreadsheet Connection

You need to be able to calculate future value on Excel – to learn how to do this, go through the work sheet 'Unit 2 Exponents and Simple Compounding in Excel'.

20. What is your entry in cell B6 of sheet 2?

21. What is your entry in cell E5 of sheet 4?

Comparing Simple and Compound Interest

You are investing $1000 with 8% interest; compare what happens if the interest is simple vs compound.

We can see that the value of your investment is greater over time when there is compound interest.

- This is not a big surprise since with compound interest you get interest on your interest, on top of what you already get with simple interest.
- Note how dramatic the increase is: after 20 years, your investment is worth over $2000 more with compound interest than with simple interest.

Year	Simple Interest	Compound Interest
1	$ 1,080.00	$ 1,080.00
2	$ 1,160.00	$ 1,166.40
3	$ 1,240.00	$ 1,259.71
4	$ 1,320.00	$ 1,360.49
5	$ 1,400.00	$ 1,469.33
6	$ 1,480.00	$ 1,586.87
7	$ 1,560.00	$ 1,713.82
8	$ 1,640.00	$ 1,850.93
9	$ 1,720.00	$ 1,999.00
10	$ 1,800.00	$ 2,158.92
11	$ 1,880.00	$ 2,331.64
12	$ 1,960.00	$ 2,518.17
13	$ 2,040.00	$ 2,719.62
14	$ 2,120.00	$ 2,937.19
15	$ 2,200.00	$ 3,172.17
16	$ 2,280.00	$ 3,425.94
17	$ 2,360.00	$ 3,700.02
18	$ 2,440.00	$ 3,996.02
19	$ 2,520.00	$ 4,315.70
20	$ 2,600.00	$ 4,660.96

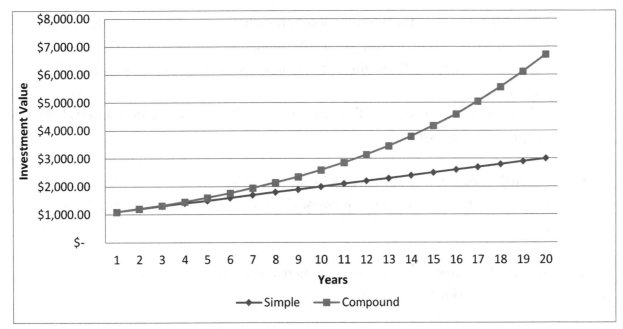

22. How would you describe the pattern of the two lines on the graph?

23. Does the difference in value between an investment with compound and simple interest increase, decrease, or stay the same over time?

24. Does the rate of change for an investment with simple interest increase, decrease, or stay the same over time?

25. Does the rate of change for an investment with compound interest increase, decrease, or stay the same over time?

The crucial difference is that with simple interest, each year you add $r \cdot PV$ to the previous total, while with compound interest, you *multiply* the previous total by $(1+r)$.

- Since we are repeatedly **adding** when dealing with **simple interest,** there is **linear growth.**
- Since we are repeatedly **multiplying** when dealing with **compound interest,** there is **exponential growth.**

Linear growth occurs if a value increases by adding a constant amount each period. **Exponential growth** occurs if a value increases by multiplying by a constant ratio each period.

You are offered an investment with simple interest at a rate of 10%, or compound interest at a rate of 8.5%. You have $9000 to invest.

26. Fill in the table for the value of your investment over 10 years, for each option.

Year	Simple Interest	Compound Interest
1		
2		
3		
4		
5		
6		
7		
8		
9		
10		

27. Sketch a graph showing the values of the two potential investments over time; it does not have to be precise.

28. For what periods of investment (if any) would the simple interest option be better? For what periods of investment (if any) would the compound interest option be better?

Note: No matter how much greater the interest rate is for simple interest is than the rate for compound interest, eventually the investment with compound interest will outgrow the one with simple interest.

- This is because an exponential function will always outgrow a linear function eventually.

Unit 2 Topic 2 Check for Understanding

Section 1. Complete the following definitions:

[Word Bank: longer, exponential, greater, compound, smaller, simple, linear, interest]

1. _Simple_ interest is when you only earn interest on the initial amount you invested.

2. When compounding over multiple years you can earn interest on your _Compound_.

3. An investment with simple interest has _linear_ growth while an investment with compound interest has _exponential_ growth.

4. With compound interest, the longer you invest for, the _greater_ the interest earned at the end of the final year.

Section 2. Simple Interest. Show all work.

5. Calculate the interest that will accrue when $600 is borrowed for one year with a simple interest rate of 8%.

$$(\omega) \ 600 (1 + .08) = \$648$$

6. Karen borrowed $2,500 from her brother to help her put a down payment on an apartment. She agreed to repay her brother in two years with 5% simple interest. How much will Karen owe her brother in two years?

$$Fv = 2500 (1 + .05(2)) = \$2750$$

7. Sarah deposits $1300 in a savings account with an interest rate of 1.2%. How much does she have after 4 years with simple interest?

$$Fv = 1300 (1 + .012(4)) = \$1362.40$$

8. Milo has $4200 to invest and aims to have $5500 in 5 years' time. What simple interest rate would he need to achieve this?

$$5500 = 4200(1 + 5r) \qquad \frac{5500}{4200} \qquad \frac{55}{42} = 1 + 5r$$
$$\frac{55}{42} - \frac{42}{42} = \frac{13}{42} = 5r \cdot \frac{1}{5} \qquad \frac{13}{42} \cdot \frac{1}{5} = r \qquad r = .06 = \boxed{6\%}$$

9. Paolo has $6250 after investing for 3 years with a simple interest rate of 3.6%. How much did he initially invest?

$$6250 = P(1 + 3(.036)) \qquad P = 5640.79 = 5640.80$$
$$\frac{6250 = P(1.108)}{1.108}$$

Section 3. Compound Interest. Show all work.

10. Kelly invests $25,000 for 15 years with compound interest at a rate of 6.26%. What is the future value of her investment?

$$Fv = P(1 + r)^t \qquad 25000(1 + .0626)^{15}$$
$$Fv = 62156.59$$

11. Geoff deposits $1750 in a savings account with an interest rate of 2.9%. How much does he have after 4 years with compounding?

$$Fv = 1750(1 + .029)^4$$
$$Fv = 1962 \text{ dollars}$$

12. Dan borrows $800 with an interest rate of 11%. How much does he owe after 3 years with compounding?

$$Fv = 800(1 + .11)^3$$
$$Fv = 1094 \text{ dollars}$$

13. Sara invests $5000 with an interest rate of 4.5%. She also takes out a loan for $1900 with an interest rate of 10.4%. Both are subject to compound interest for five years.
    a. What is the future value of the investment?

$$Fv = 5000(1 + .045)^5 \qquad\qquad Fv = 1900(1 + .104)^5$$
$$Fv = 46230.50 \qquad\qquad Fv = \$3116.$$

b. What is the future value of the loan?

$$FV = 1900(1+.104)^5$$

$$= \$3116$$

c. What is Sara's net income over five years (ignoring all other transactions)?

$$\$6230.9 - 3116.01$$

$$= \$3114.9$$

d. Suppose Sara had not taken out the loan and instead had invested $1900 less. What would her net income have been then? In light of this, what advice would you offer Sara?

$$FV = 3100(1+.045)^5$$

$$= \$3863.16$$

Section 4

You are offered an investment with simple interest at a rate of 15%, or compound interest at a rate of 13%. You have $9000 to invest.

14. Fill in the table for the value of you investment over 10 years, for each option.

Year	Simple Interest	Compound Interest
1		
2		
3		
4		
5		
6		
7		
8		
9		
10		

15. Sketch a graph showing the values of the two potential investments over time.

16. For what periods of investment (if any) would the simple interest option be better? For what periods of investment (if any) would the compound interest option be better?

 Extension

17. Jennifer wants to invest $3000 and aims to have at least $3700 in 3 years' time. With compounding, what interest rate would she need to achieve this?

 Spreadsheet Connection

Now complete 'Unit 2 Topic 2 Check Sheet'.

32

TOPIC 3: THE COMPOUND INTEREST FORMULA

So far, we have assumed that interest is paid all at once at the end of each year. Sometimes, though, it is paid in *installments*: monthly, weekly, or daily.

Often it is paid in equal amounts over the course of the year.

Example: If an investment pays $60 in interest over a year with monthly payments, each month it will pay $60/12 = $5

Generally, if there are *n* interest payments over a year, each payment will be equal to the total interest for the year divided by *n*.

1. An investment pays $104 over a year with weekly payments. What is the value of each payment?

2. You invest $2000 with an interest rate of 9%, and receive quarterly payments. What is the value of each payment?

We can also calculate the **total value** of an investment at various points in the year.

Example: You invest $900 in an account with an interest rate of 8% that makes quarterly payments.
- Your total interest for the year is 900*0.08 = 72
- The payment each quarter is 72/4 = 18
- Therefore, after one quarter, the total value of your investment will be 900 + 18 = 918
- After two quarters, the total value of your investment will be 900 + 18*2 = 936
- After three quarters, the total value of your investment will be 900 + 18*3 = 954
- After four quarters (i.e. one year), the total value of your investment will be 900 + 18*4 = 972
  - This matches our original calculation that you receive $72 interest over the year.

3. You invest $360 with an interest rate of 6% and receive monthly payments. What is the value of your investment after three months?

Now consider the general case where you have an investment with present value PV, which earns interest at rate r, and has n payments within a year. We want to calculate the value of the investment at any point during the year, after t payments have been made.

Formula	Explanation
$PV \bullet r$	This is the total interest you earn over the year.
$PV \bullet \dfrac{r}{n}$	This is the value of each payment – the total interest divided by the number of payments.
$PV \bullet \dfrac{r}{n} \cdot t$	This is the interest you receive from t payments.
$PV + PV \bullet \dfrac{r}{n} \cdot t$ $PV(1 + \dfrac{r}{n} \cdot t)$	This is the total value of your investment after t payments. We simplify by factoring out PV.

Recall the **simple interest formula** $FV = PV \bullet (1 + rt)$. Notice that this is the same as the formula we just derived if you replace r with r/n.

- This is because each payment is r/n of the initial value of the investment.
- Since each payment is a fixed percentage of the present value, they are in effect a series on simple interest payments.
- This gives us the following formula:

Simple interest within a year: $FV = PV(1 + \frac{r}{n} \cdot t)$

Formula Key:

FV = Future Value

PV = Present Value

r = Rate

n = Number of payments per year

t = Number of payments received $[t \leq n]$

Note: Though simple interest doesn't often occur in the real world across multiple years, it does often occur *within* a year. For example, many bank accounts make monthly simple interest payments.

4. You have an investment of $30,000 with 7.8% interest and daily payments. How much will you have after 90 days? Make *explicit* use of the **simple interest within a year** formula.

We have seen that you can earn simple interest with a year, but you can also earn **compound interest**.

Compound Interest (within a year): You collect interest over shorter periods and reinvest, so you earn *more* interest on your interest.

- If there is a rate of 8% over the period of a year, you will earn half of the original sum in interest after half a year, i.e. 4%.

Example: You invest $1000 over two half-years, with an annual rate of 8%, which gives us $FV = 1000 \cdot \left(1 + \frac{0.08}{2}\right)^2 = 1081.60$; so compounding gets you an extra $1.60.

Speaking more generally, if there is rate r over the period of a year, you will earn $r/2$ of the original sum in interest after half a year.

- After half a year $FV = PV + PV \cdot \frac{r}{2} = PV \cdot (1 + \frac{r}{2})$
- If you reinvest after 6 months and collect interest again at the end of the year, you will earn another $\frac{r}{2}$ interest.
- Therefore $FV = PV \cdot \left(1 + \frac{r}{2}\right) + PV \cdot \left(1 + \frac{r}{2}\right) \cdot \frac{r}{2} = PV \cdot \left(1 + \frac{r}{2}\right) \cdot \left(1 + \frac{r}{2}\right) = PV \cdot (1 + \frac{r}{2})^2$

This generalizes for any number of times, n, that you reinvest over a period, giving us the formula:

$$FV = PV \cdot (1 + \frac{r}{n})^n$$

5. You invest $81 for a year with an interest rate of 4.5%, and you reinvest 4 times over the year. What is the value of your investment at the end of the year?

If you reinvest many times per year over multiple years, the interest compounds further:

Example: You invest $1000 at 8% for two years, reinvesting twice a year.

- After one year, you have $FV = 1000 \cdot \left(1 + \frac{0.08}{2}\right)^2$
- During the second year the same process applies, so you multiply the total after one year by $\left(1 + \frac{0.08}{2}\right)^2$

- This gives you FV $= 1000 \cdot \left(1 + \frac{0.08}{2}\right)^2 \cdot \left(1 + \frac{0.08}{2}\right)^2 = 1000 \cdot \left(1 + \frac{0.08}{2}\right)^4 =$ 1169.86

Now look at the general case with rate r, and n reinvestments.

- If you invest for two years, you have: $\left(FV = PV \cdot \left(1 + \frac{r}{n}\right)^n\right) \cdot \left(1 + \frac{r}{n}\right)^n = PV \cdot (1 + \frac{r}{n})^{n \cdot 2}$

- In general, for each additional year you invest, you multiply the amount you had at the start of the year by $\left(1 + \frac{r}{n}\right)^n$

- If we invest for t years, we get the following formula:

Compound interest formula: $FV = PV \cdot (1 + \frac{r}{n})^{n \cdot t}$

Formula Key:

FV = Future Value

PV = Present Value

r = Interest rate

n = Reinvestments per year

t = Years of investment

Example: You invest $450 at 7.5%. You reinvest monthly for 3 years.

- Here, $n = 12$, $t = 3$, $PV = 450$, $r = 0.075$ therefore: FV $= 450 \cdot \left(1 + \frac{0.075}{12}\right)^{12 \cdot 3} =$ 563.15

6. You invest $2450 at 9.1% and reinvest quarterly. How much will you have after four years?

As an alternative to saying you *reinvest* a number of times with a period, we often say you **compound** within a period.

- Monthly compounding means reinvesting every month.
- Quarterly compounding means reinvesting _____ times a year.

A note on Annual Compounding: In the special case where n=1, the **compound interest formula** becomes $FV = PV \cdot (1 + \frac{r}{1})^{1 \cdot t}$, which simplifies to $FV = PV \cdot (1 + r)^t$

- This shows that the simple compounding formula discussed in topic 2 is just a special case of the compound interest formula when n=1.

Spreadsheet Connection

It's important to use in the compound interest formula in spreadsheets too. Go through the material and questions in the worksheet 'Unit 2 Topic 3 Compound Interest Formula' to learn how to do this.

Comparing Simple and Compound Interest (within a year)

We can compare how the value of an investment changes over time depending on if there's simple or compound interest **within** a year (while in both cases there is compound interest **across** years).

Consider an investment with a principal of $1000 and interest rate of 10%. Compare what happens if there is monthly compounding each month vs simple interest payments each month.

Here is the value of interest earned over a year:

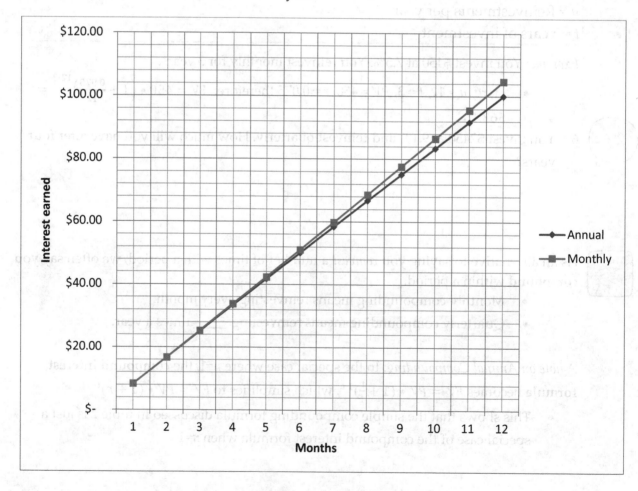

You can see that you earn more interest with monthly compounding.

- They increase at the same amount in the first month, but after that the simple interest value increases linearly while the compound interest increases exponentially.
- This means that the gap between the two values increases with each month.

Now look what happens to the values over multiple years:

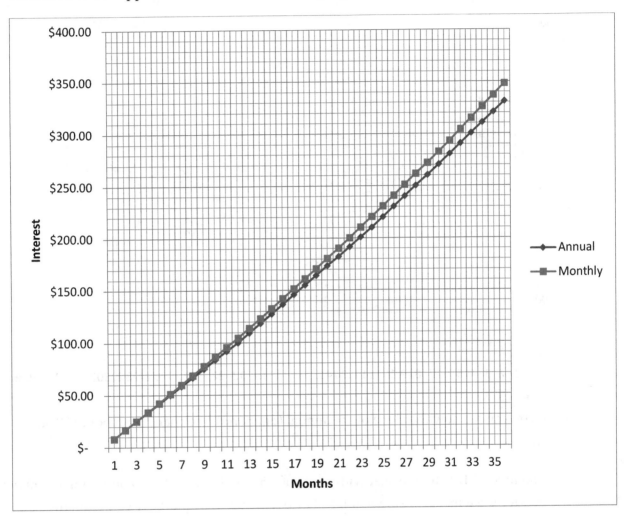

We can see that the gap between the two keeps on increasing, but not as rapidly as in the graph of page 19.

- This is because the simple interest investment doesn't continue to increase **linearly**: at the end of each year the slope increases, due to the annual compounding.

This is hard to see on the graph above, but is more apparent if we imagine a case with very high interest – below is a graph where the interest rate is 50% (something that never happens in real life).

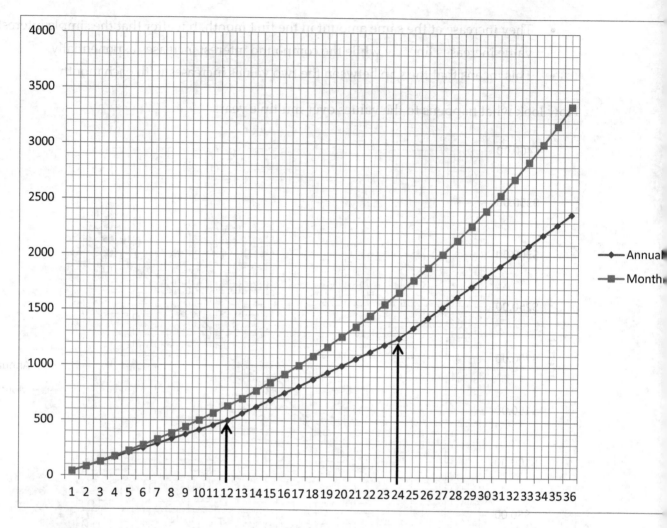

Here you can see how the slope of the annual (diamond) line changes at month 12 and month 24.

7. You invest $12,000 for a year with a rate of 4.5%. Fill out the table comparing if you have quarterly payments of simple interest or payments with quarterly compounding.

Quarter of Investment	Value with simple interest	Value with compounding
1		
2		
3		
4		

Euler's Number

Math Check

To understand the material in the next section, you must be comfortable with Euler's number, e. You should know:

- e is the name of a special constant. It's an irrational number that we represent with a letter similar to π.
- Its approximate value: $e \cong 2.718$
- It's on your calculator. Can you find it?
- See this video for an introduction to e:
  https://www.khanacademy.org/math/algebra2/exponential-and-logarithmic-functions/e-and-the-natural-logarithm/v/e-as-limit
- See this video for some applications of e:
  https://www.youtube.com/watch?v=b-MZumVocabularybt8

8. Write down e to 8 decimal places:

   2.71828183

9. Write down e^3 to 4 decimal places:

   20.0855

Extension

Consider the sequence: $(1 + \frac{1}{1})^1$, $(1 + \frac{1}{2})^2$, $(1 + \frac{1}{3})^3$, $(1 + \frac{1}{4})^4$, ...

10. Evaluate the first five terms in this sequence.

$$\left(1 + \frac{1}{5}\right)^5$$

Notice that each term in the series is bigger than the last. Indeed, for any n, $(1 + \frac{1}{n+1})^{n+1} > (1 + \frac{1}{n})^n$

- Does this mean the sequence will continue to grow to any number we desire given a big enough n?

  No

11. Evaluate $(1 + \frac{1}{n})^n$ to 4 decimal places for $n = 20, 50, 1000$. What do you notice?

   2.6512   2.6915   2.717

40

As n get bigger, $(1 + \frac{1}{n})^n$ gets closer and closer to a particular number: e. We say that e is the **limit** of the sequence.

- Alternatively, we can write: $\lim_{n \to \infty} \left(1 + \frac{1}{n}\right)^n = e$, which means that e is the limit reached when 'n approaches infinity'.

Continuous Compounding

We saw that reinvesting a small number of times gets you more interest: What happens if you keep reinvesting?

- Note that $FV = PV \cdot (1 + \frac{r}{n+1})^{n+1} > FV = PV \cdot (1 + \frac{r}{n})^n$ so the more times you reinvest, the more interest you earn.
- Does this mean you can turn your investment into a fortune if you reinvest frequently enough?

Return to our example of investing $1000 at 8% interest for one year.

- The table shows what happens as we increase the number of reinvestments

Though FV keeps increasing, the amount it increases by gets smaller and smaller as n increases.

- FV will never reach $1083.30, however many times you reinvest
- Mathematically speaking, there is a **limit** to the value of FV as n increases
- This limit is the maximum amount of interest that can be earned through compounding – reaching the limit is known as **continuous compounding.**

n	FV
1	1080.00
2	1081.60
4	1082.43
8	1082.86
16	1083.07
32	1083.18
64	1083.23
128	1083.26
256	1083.27
512	1083.28
1024	1083.28
2048	1083.29

 Interest with **continuous compounding** refers to the amount of interest you get if you take the limit of the amount you get from compounding as many times as possible.

Example: As we saw above, if you invest $1000 for a year with an interest rate of 8%, the amount you get with **continuous compounding** is approximately $1080.30.

We can calculate interest with continuous compounding using the formula below.

Continuous compounding formula: $FV = PV \cdot e^{rt}$

Formula Key:

FV = Future Value
PV = Present Value
r = Interest rate
t = Periods of investment
e = Euler's number

Example: You invest $1000 with 8% interest and continuous compounding. After a year we get $FV = 1000 \bullet e^{0.08} \cong 1083.29$

- Continuous compounding gets you an additional $3.29
- Since $e^{0.08} \cong 1.08329$, continuously compounding a rate of 8% is equivalent to a simple interest rate of 8.329%

12. You invest $538 at a rate of 4.2% with continuous compounding. How much will you have after five years?

13. You invest $2540 at a rate of 7.8% for 10 years. How much more will you earn if there is continuous compounding? What would be the difference if you had annual compounding?

Extension

Where does the **continuous compounding formula** come from?

We know that continuous compounding is the **limit** for the value of an investment when you compound as frequently as possible.
- We can put it symbolically using an investment with present value PV, future value FV, interest rate r, and number of times compounding n.
- The compound interest formula tells us $FV = PV \left(1 + \frac{r}{n}\right)^n$
- Therefore, continuous compounding is the limit as n gets really big for $PV \left(1 + \frac{r}{n}\right)^n$
- Using mathematical notation, we say $FV = \lim\limits_{n\to\infty} \left(1 + \frac{r}{n}\right)^n$
- We know that $e = \lim\limits_{n\to\infty} \left(1 + \frac{1}{n}\right)^n$ which looks kind of like the formula above – however, there's an r in the numerator of the fraction that isn't there in the definition of e. We have to rearrange the continuous compounding formula so that it matches the definition.
- $FV = \lim\limits_{n\to\infty} \left(1 + \frac{r}{n}\right)^n = \lim\limits_{n\to\infty} \left(1 + \frac{1}{\frac{n}{r}}\right)^n = \lim\limits_{n\to\infty} \left(1 + \frac{1}{\frac{n}{r}}\right)^{\left(\frac{n}{r}\right)*r} = \lim\limits_{n\to\infty} \left(\left(1 + \frac{1}{\left(\frac{n}{r}\right)}\right)^{\left(\frac{n}{r}\right)}\right)^r$
- If we replace n with n/r, we now have the formula for e^r (allowing for the fact that as n goes to infinity, so does n/r)
- This tells us that $FV = PV \cdot e^r$, i.e. the **continuous compounding formula**

Comparing Varieties of Compounding

This graph shows interest earned over a year with an investment of $1000 and rate of 10%, relative to different kinds of compounding.

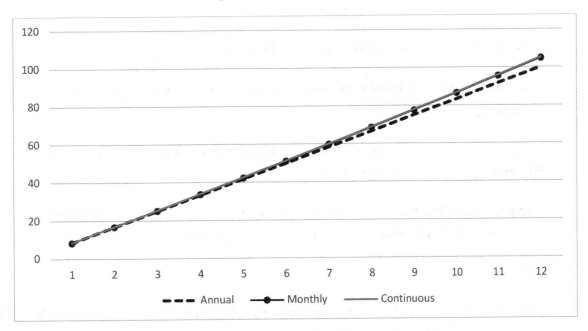

You can see that the bottom line for annual compounding is below the other two. You might not be able to see it on this diagram but continuous compounding earns slightly more than monthly compounding. It's clearer though in the graph below that uses the artificial interest rate of 50% so that all three lines can clearly be distinguished.

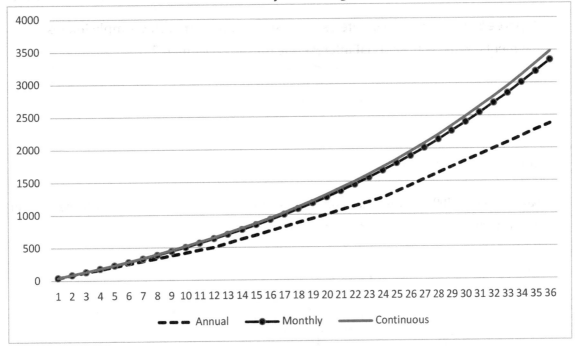

Unit 2 Topic 3 Check for Understanding

Section 1:

Fill in the blanks using the word bank:

[Word Bank: ultimate, square, decreases, limit, increases, continuous]

1. When you increase the number of times you reinvest over a single period, the interest you earn _____.

2. The maximum amount of interest earned through reinvesting within a period is obtained with _____ compounding.

3. You get the continuous compounding formula by taking the _____ of the series as you increase the number of times you reinvest in a period.

Section 2:

4. Calculate the future value of a $1,200 after 9 months, when there is an interest rate of 7% with monthly simple interest payments.

5. Suppose $1,000 earns $85 in interest after six months of monthly simple interest payments. What is the annual interest rate for the investment?

Section 3:

6. Sally invests $4000. There is an annual interest rate of 6%; how much will she have after a year if there is monthly compounding?

7. Xiao wants to invest $23,000 in an account with an annual interest rate of 7.9%. How much extra will he have after a year if he compounds daily, instead of collecting simple interest?

Section 4:

8. You invest $3000 for three years with an interest rate of 5%. How much do you have at the end of three years if:

   a. You only collect simple interest

   b. You compound annually

   c. You compound monthly

   d. You compound daily

   e. You compound continuously

46

9. You are planning to invest $5000 for four years in an account that offers interest at 6.3% compounding annually. However, you find out you can pay $100 to have your investment compound continuously. Should you take this offer?

10. Michael has $2200 to invest and the best annual interest rate he can find is 5.9%. He wants to have a total of at least $3000 after one year. He has the option to compound as many times as he likes within the period. Is it possible for him to meet his goal? Explain your answer.

11. Ginger invests $11,300 for 6 years with an annual interest rate of 4.7% with continuous compounding. How much money does she have after the six-year investment?

12. You invest $2590 for a year with a rate of 7.2%.

    a. Fill out the table comparing if you have monthly payments of simple interest, payments with monthly compounding, or payments with continuous compounding.

Month of Investment	Value with Simple Interest	Value with Monthly Compounding	Value with Continuous Compounding
1			
2			
3			
4			
5			
6			
7			
8			
9			
10			
11			
12			

    b. If you were compounding annually, what interest rate would you need to do better than a loan with 7.2% interest and monthly compounding? Explain your answer.

 Spreadsheet Connection

Now, complete the spreadsheet questions on 'Unit 2 Topic 3 Check Sheet'.

48

Extension

The three lines on this graph represent interest earned per month for investments with three different kinds of compounding. What kind of compounding applies to each line? Explain your answer. (*Hint*: Focus on the *shapes and order* of the lines, you don't need to make any calculations.)

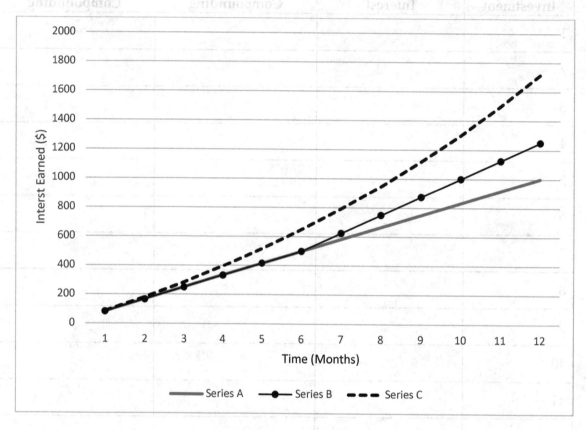

TOPIC 4: THE RULE OF 72 – DOUBLE YOUR MONEY

To understand the material in this topic, you must be comfortable with logs – check your knowledge with the questions below.

Math Check 2: Properties of Logs

Definition: $\log_c a = b$ is an equivalent statement to $c^b = a$

- In order to get a, you have to raise c to the power b

Examples:

- $\log_3 9 = 2$, since $3^2 = 9$
- $\log_2 8 = 3$, since $2^3 = 8$

You will need to use the following properties of logs to answer the questions below:

1) $\text{Log}_c \, A \bullet B$	=	$\text{Log}_c \, A + \text{Log}_c \, B$
2) $\text{Log}_c \, A/B$	=	$\text{Log}_c \, A - \text{Log}_c \, B$
3) $\text{Log}_c \, A^B$	=	$B \bullet \text{Log}_c \, A$
4) $\text{Log}_A \, (A)$	=	1
5) $\text{Log}_A \, (1)$	=	0
6) $\text{Log}_A \, (A^x)$	=	X

1. Write the following in exponential form:

   a. $log_4 256 = x$

   $$4^x = 256$$

   b. $log_9 81 = a$

   $$9^a = 81$$

2. Write the following in logarithmic form:

   a. $3^x = 81$

   $$\log_3 81 = x$$

   b. $8^x = 512$

   $$\log_8 512 = x$$

3. Evaluate:

   a. $log_7 343$ $= 3$

   b. $log_5 625$ $= 4$

50

c. $\log_6 6^{3.3} = 3.3$

d. $\log 1,000,000$ = 6

e. $\log_{2.7} 2.7$
   1

f. $\log_{85} 1$ = 0

4. Convert to Scientific Notation:

   a. 704,000,000
      7.04×10^8

   b. 83,100,000,000
      8.31×10^{10}

   c. 0.000867
      8.67×10^{-4}

   d. 432.6
      4.326×10^2

5. Calculate:

   a. $(1.13 \cdot 10^7)(2 \cdot 10^{11})$

   b. $(8.3 \cdot 10^6)(3 \cdot 10^{22})$

   c. $(7 \cdot 10^5)(6 \cdot 10^{13})$

   d. $(3.3 \cdot 10^{51})(1 \cdot 10^9)$

6. Calculate:

   a. $\log (1.79 \cdot 10^9)$

   b. $\log (9.3 \cdot 10^{10})$

   c. $\log (2.15 \cdot 10^{31})$

   d. $\log (4.2 \cdot 10^{17})$

7. Calculate:

   a. $\log (2,850,000)$

   b. $\log (990,000,000,000,000,000)$

c. log (315)   d. log (4.4)

8. Natural Logs

Natural Log refers to the log with base *e* (Euler's number). This tells us:

$ln(A)$	=	$Log_e(A)$
$ln(e)$	=	1
e^{lnB}	=	B

9. Write the following in exponential form:

a. $ln\,10 = x$

$e^x = 10$

b. $ln\,a^b = c$

$e^c = a^b$

10. Write the following in logarithmic form:

a. $e^x = 81$

$ln\,81 = x$

b. $e^x = \pi$

$ln\,\pi = x$

11. Evaluate:

a. $ln\,343$ = 5.838

b. $ln\,625$ 6.438

c. $ln\,e^{3.3}$ = 3.3

d. $ln\,1,000,000$ = 13.816

52

 Extension

VIII. Challenges:

 12. $\log_4 0.456$ 13. $\log_9(81^5)$ 14. $\log(10^7) \cdot \log(10^{0.5})$ 14. $\log(0.0000178)$

IX. Explaining:

Givens:

a. $\log(A \cdot B) = \log(A) + \log(B)$

b. Multiplication is repeated addition. $A \bullet B = \underbrace{A + A \ldots + A}$

> A added to itself B times

c. Exponentiation is repeated Multiplication: $A \bullet B = \underbrace{A \bullet A \ldots A \bullet A}$

> A multiplied by itself B times

15. Explain why the following statement is true. Feel free to use examples, notes, pictures or anything else you think might help in your explanation.

$$\log(A^B) = B \cdot \log(A)$$

16. Explain why the properties of logs listed at the start of this worksheet are true. Use the fact that a logarithm is the *inverse* of exponentiation: that is, $A^{\log_A B} = B$

Simple to Continuous Compounding

Example: You are offered 5% interest on your $1000 savings with simple compounding. In order to compare this offer with other options, you need to calculate the equivalent rate of interest with continuous compounding.

- What interest rate with continuous compounding offers the same future value as 5% with simple compounding?

We can use natural logs to move between simple compound interest and continuously compounded interest, in order to answer this question.

- With simple compounding at 5%: $FV = PV \bullet (1.05)^t$
- With continuous compounding at rate r: $FV = PV \bullet e^{rt}$
- In order for these to be equal, $e^{rt} = (1.05)^t$, therefore $e^r = 1.05$.
- By taking the natural log (ln) of both sides of the equation we can see that this equation holds when $r = \ln(1.05) = 0.0488$.

17. Verify with your calculator that if you invest $1000 for 4 years with simple compounding at 5%, you end up with (approximately) the same amount as if you invest $1000 for 4 years with continuous compounding at 4.88%. Write down the values displayed on your calculator in each case.

We can also do this in reverse, to find the simple compounding rate equivalent to a given continuous compounding rate.

Example: You are offered 3% interest on your $1000 savings with continuous compounding. You want to know what the equivalent rate of interest would be with simple compounding.

- This means that for simple interest rate R, $FV = PV \bullet e^{0.03 \cdot t} = PV \bullet (1 + R)^t$
- Therefore, $1 + R = e^{0.03}$, so $R = e^{0.03} - 1 = 0.0304$

Notice that these two equations are equivalent: $1 + R = e^r$ if and only if $r = \ln(1 + R)$

54

This gives us the following formula:

Simple Compounding to Continuous Compounding:
Suppose that $r = \ln(1 + R)$ or $R = e^r - 1$; then the following holds:

$$PV \cdot e^{rt} = PV \cdot (1 + R)^t$$

Formula Key:
FV = Future Value
PV = Present Value
r = Interest rate with continuous compounding
R = Interest rate with simple compounding
t = Periods of investment

Example: Janet is offered an interest rate of 2.5% with simple compounding. What is the equivalent rate with continuous compounding?
- We know that $R = 0.025$
- $r = \ln(1 + R) = \ln 1.025 = 0.0247$
- Therefore, the equivalent rate with continuous compounding is 2.47%

Example: Terry is offered an interest rate of 19% for a loan with continuous compounding. Calculate the equivalent rate with simple compounding.
- We know that $r = 0.19$
- $R = e^r - 1 = e^{0.19} - 1 = 0.209$
- Therefore, the equivalent rate with simple compounding is 20.9%

18. Ava is offered an interest rate of 7.7% for her savings with simple compounding. Calculate the equivalent rate with continuous compounding.

$$r = .077$$
$$r = \ln(1 + R) \quad e^{.077} \quad \ln 1.077 = \qquad 7.42\%$$
$$= 0.0742$$

19. Marco is offered an interest rate of 8.2% for a loan with continuous compounding. Calculate the equivalent rate with simple compounding.

$$r = .082$$
$$e^{.082} - 1 = 0.0855$$
$$8.55\%$$

Spreadsheet CONNECTION

You can move between simple and continuous compounding on a spreadsheet too. Go through 'Unit 2 Topic 4 Simple to Continuous Compounding' to learn how to do this.

Rule of 72

It's useful to know how long it will take for an investment to double in value.
- We want to know when $FV = 2 \bullet PV$
- This allows you to make a quick estimate as to the value of an investment after a certain period of time.

20. You invest $4000, and your investment will double in value every 5 years. How much will you have after 20 years?

You can work out how long it takes to double your money using the **Rule of 72**.
- This says that if you divide 72 by the interest rate (as a percentage), you will get the approximate number of periods it takes to double your money.
- This is shown mathematically below.

Rule of 72: $t = \dfrac{72}{R \cdot 100}$

Formula Key:

FV = Future Value
PV = Present Value
R = Interest rate with simple compounding
t = Periods of investment required for you to double your money

---

Note: If we take R as a percentage, and ignore the percentage sign, we can simplify to: $t = \dfrac{72}{R}$

Example: You invest $425 with an interest rate of 12%, how long will it take for you to double your money?
- This means that $R=0.12$, therefore, $t = \dfrac{72}{0.12 \cdot 100} = \dfrac{72}{12} = 6$
- We can verify this by calculating future value after 6 years, $FV = 425 \bullet (1.12)^6 = 838.9$ – this is *approximately* double 425
- Note that if we take R as a percentage, we can use $t = \dfrac{72}{R} = \dfrac{72}{12} = 6$ (and the answers match)

21. If you're investing $39 with an interest rate of 3.2%, how long, approximately, will it take you to double you money? Verify your answer by calculating FV directly.

22. Complete the table:

    a. First, enter the approximate time for an investment or loan to double with the interest rate in the left-hand column.

    b. Then, in the right-hand column, calculate the actual future value (as a multiple of the present value) after the time you derived using the **compound interest formula**.

Note: The rule of 72 still applies when 72/r is not a whole number – just round the result up or down.

Interest Rate	Approximate time to double (t)	Actual Value after time t
1%	72/1 = 72	$FV = PV(1.01)^{72} = 2.05PV$
2%		
3%		
4%		
5%		
6%		
7%		
8%		
9%		
10%		
11%		
12%		
15%		
20%		
25%		

Note: The rule of 72 provides a useful way to **estimate** the value of investments and loans.

Example 1: You invest $500 with an interest rate of 6%. Estimate how much your investment will be worth after 24 years.

- By the rule of 72, we know that with a rate of 6% your money doubles every 12 years, since 72/6=12
- Since 24=12·2, your investment will double twice over 24 years.
- Therefore, the value of your investment will be approximately 500·2·2=2000

Example 2: You take out a loan for $2100 with an interest rate of 9%. If you don't make any payments, how long will it be until you owe $4200?

- Since $4200 is double $2100, we need to estimate how long it will take to double the value of the loan.
- With a rate of 9%, the rule of 72 tells us it takes 8 years to double your money.
- Therefore, the value of your loan will be approximately $4200 after 8 years.

Directions: Make sure to estimate when answering. If possible, do not use a calculator.

23. You take out a loan for $5000 with a rate of 7.2%. If you don't make any payments, how much will you owe after 20 years?

24. You invest $25,000 with an interest rate of 3%. How long will it be until your investment is worth $200,000?

25. You invest $400 with an interest rate of 2%. Your accountant tells you that after 20 years, your investment will be worth $1000. Without calculating the future value yourself, can you tell if your accountant's claim is reasonable? Explain your answer.

Example 3: You invest $1900. What interest rate do you need to in order to double your money in 9 years?

- We can find the answer to this by *rearranging* the rule of 72 equation and solving for R.
- If $t = \frac{72}{R \cdot 100}$, then $R = \frac{72}{t \cdot 100}$
- Substituting in our values: $R = \frac{72}{9 \cdot 100} = 0.08$

26. What interest rate do you need if you want to double your money in 14 years?

27. You invest $5600 and want to have $22400 in 10 years. What interest rate do you need for this?

Extension

Deriving the rule - Where does the rule of 72 come from?

We have a pair of equations: $FV=2 \bullet PV$ and $FV = PV \bullet (1 + R)^t$

- We want to use these to derive a simple relationship between t and R.
- We do this using what we know about the connection between simple and continuous compounding.

Formula	Comment
$FV = 2 \bullet PV$	This is the equation we assume is true.
$FV = PV \bullet (1 + R)^t$	We know this equation holds given the **compound interest formula**.
$FV = PV \bullet e^{\ln(1+R) \cdot t}$	We know this must also hold given the **simple compounding to continuous compounding** formula.
$2 \bullet PV = PV \bullet e^{\ln(1+R) \cdot t}$	We want to find a relationship between R and t, so we need to eliminate FV and PV. To do this, we first substitute 2PV for FV since we know they are identical.
$2 = e^{\ln(1+R) \cdot t}$	We can remove PV as a common factor to get this equation.
$\ln 2 = \ln \left(e^{\ln(1+R) \cdot t}\right)$	We get the following equation by taking the natural log of both sides
$\ln 2 = \ln(1 + R) \cdot t$	We simplify the right-hand side using the fact that $\ln(e^x) = x$
$t = \dfrac{\ln 2}{\ln(1 + R)}$	Now we rearrange to solve for t
$\ln 2 \approx 0.72$ $\ln(1 + R) \approx R$, when R is small	We use the following two facts about natural logs: verify with your calculator or see the table below
$t = \dfrac{0.72}{R}$	We substitute 0.72 for ln2 and R for ln(1+R) to arrive at the final formula.

Note: The reason we use 0.72 as an approximation for ln2 rather than 0.7 is that 72 has many more factors than 70, which makes for a rule that can be used for quicker mental calculations.

R=0.01	ln(1 + R)=0.00995
R=0.03	ln(1 + R)=0.0296
R=0.05	ln(1 + R)=0.0488
R=0.1	ln(1 + R)=0.0953

28. Use the same method to come up with a rule to tell you approximately how long it will take to *triple* your money.

Converting other kinds of Compounding (Extension)

We know how to move from a simple interest rate to the equivalent rate with continuous compounding, but what about monthly compounding? Or quarterly compounding?

Suppose we earn interest at rate r, with compounding n times per year, and we want to know the equivalent rate with annual compounding.

- We know that with compounding n times per year, $FV = PV \cdot (1 + \frac{r}{n})^{n \cdot t}$
- We also know that with annual compounding, $FV = PV \cdot (1 + R)^t$

Therefore, we want to find an R such that the following equation holds:

- $PV \cdot \left(1 + \frac{r}{n}\right)^{n \cdot t} = PV \cdot (1 + R)^t$
- Or to simplify: $\left(1 + \frac{r}{n}\right)^{n} = 1 + R$
- Now we just need to solve for R by subtracting one from both sides of our equation.

> To convert from a rate (r) with compounding n times a year to rate with annual compounding (R):
>
> $$R = \left(1 + \frac{r}{n}\right)^{n} - 1$$

Example: If you earn interest at a rate of 6% with quarterly compounding, what is the equivalent rate with annual compounding?

- We know $r = 0.06$ and $n = 4$
- Therefore, $R = \left(1 + \frac{r}{n}\right)^{n} - 1 = \left(1 + \frac{0.06}{4}\right)^{4} - 1 = 0.0614$, or 6.14%

What if you know the rate with annual compounding and want to find out the equivalent rate with compounding n times per year.

- In this case we need to solve the following equation for little r : $\left(1 + \frac{r}{n}\right)^{n} = 1 + R$
- This gives us: $r = \left((1 + R)^{\frac{1}{n}} - 1\right) \cdot n$

To convert from a rate with annual compounding (R) to a rate (r) with compounding n times a year:

- $r = \left((1 + R)^{\frac{1}{n}} - 1\right) \cdot n$

Note: $x^{\frac{1}{n}}$ is another way of writing the nth root of x.

Example: If you earn interest at a rate of 8% with annual compounding, what is the equivalent rate with monthly compounding?

- We know $R = 0.08$ and $n = 12$
- Therefore, $r = ((1 + R)^{\frac{1}{n}} - 1) \cdot n = ((1 + 0.08)^{\frac{1}{12}} - 1) \cdot 12 = 0.0772$, or 7.72%

29. If you earn interest at a rate of 2.4% with monthly compounding, what is the equivalent rate with annual compounding?

30. If you earn interest at a rate of 15% with daily compounding, what is the equivalent rate with annual compounding?

31. If you earn interest at a rate of 5.9% with annual compounding, what is the equivalent rate with semi-annual compounding?

32. If you earn interest at a rate of 9.2% with annual compounding, what is the equivalent rate with weekly compounding?

33. If you earn interest at a rate of 6.35% with monthly compounding, what is the equivalent rate with *continuous* compounding? (*Hint*: Try calculating the rate with annual compounding first.)

Unit 2 Topic 4 Check for Understanding

Section 1

[Word Bank: crush; double; shrink; $\ln(1 + R)$; e^R]

1. The rule of 72 tells you how long it takes to _____ your money.

2. We know that when $r = \ln(1 + R)$, $PV \cdot e^{rt} = PV \cdot (1 + R)^t$. This tells us that continuously compounding at rate ____ is equivalent to annually compounding at rate R.

3. The rule of 72 tells us that to find out how long it takes to double your money you must

   _____.

   (fill in the blank by circling the correct answer below)

   a. Wait 72 years
   b. Divide 72 by the percentage interest rate
   c. Take the interest rate as a decimal and multiply it by 72
   d. Divide the dollar amount you invest by 72

4. The rule of 72 is useful because: (circle the answers that apply, there may be more than one)

   a. It allows you to get a quick estimate of the future value of an investment or loan
   b. Bankers don't let you use calculators in front of them, so you need to be able to make calculations in your head
   c. Knowing precise numbers is for nerds so it's better to only know the rough future value
   d. Using the rule gives you a quick way to check whether a financial calculation is off the mark

Section 2

5. What simple interest rate is equivalent to investing at a rate of 7% continuously compounded?

6. What interest rate with continuous compounding is equivalent to investing with simple compounding at a 4.35% rate?

Section 3

In answering these questions, use the rule of 72 to make an estimate. If possible, don't use a calculator.

7. If you invest with an interest rate of 4%, how long will it take you to double your money?

8. You invest $2000 with an interest rate of 5.2%. How long will it take for your investment to be valued at $8000?

9. You take out a loan for $9900 with a rate of 14.4%. If you don't make any payments, how much will you owe after 15 years?

10. You invest $2000 with an interest rate of 12%. How long will it be until your investment is worth $128,000?

11. You borrow $3000 with an interest rate of 10%. Your accountant tells you that after 8 years, your investment will be $4500. Without calculating the future value yourself, can you tell if your accountant's claim is reasonable? Explain your answer.

64

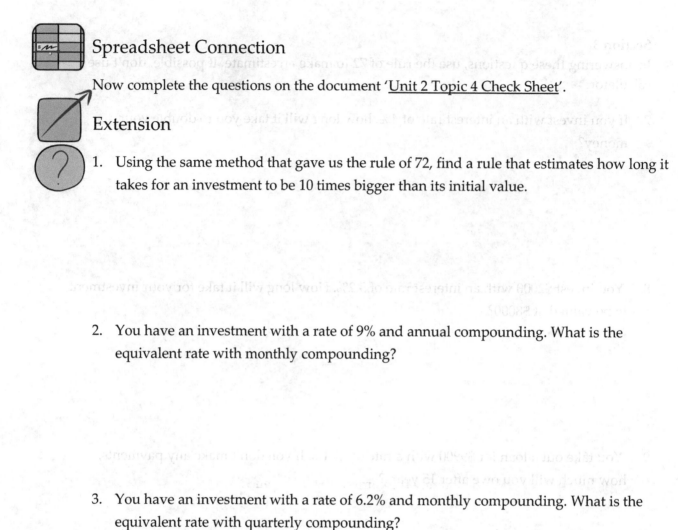

Spreadsheet Connection

Now complete the questions on the document 'Unit 2 Topic 4 Check Sheet'.

Extension

1. Using the same method that gave us the rule of 72, find a rule that estimates how long it takes for an investment to be 10 times bigger than its initial value.

2. You have an investment with a rate of 9% and annual compounding. What is the equivalent rate with monthly compounding?

3. You have an investment with a rate of 6.2% and monthly compounding. What is the equivalent rate with quarterly compounding?

4. You make a very fortunate investment which has an interest rate of 80%! Can you use the rule of 72 here? Explain your answer.

TOPIC 5: PRESENT VALUE

With compounding we calculated how much a dollar invested now would be worth at a given time in the future.

- Sometimes we want to know to how much a dollar paid in the future is worth now.
- For example: You may have a target sum of money you want saved when you retire, and you want to know much you'd have to invest now to achieve that in 20 years' time.

When you know the future value of an investment or loan, you need to calculate the present value.

1. Can you think of a scenario in which you would need to calculate the present value, given the future value? Or a situation in which it might be helpful to do so?

Discounting is the process of calculating the present value of a given sum paid in the future.

- We can do this by rearranging the compounding formula.
- We know that $FV = PV \bullet (1 + \frac{r}{n})^{n \cdot t}$
- We can solve for PV dividing both sides by $(1 + \frac{r}{n})^{n \cdot t}$
- Therefore $PV = \frac{FV}{(1 + \frac{r}{n})^{n \cdot t}}$
- Using the rules of exponents, we can rewrite this formula as $PV = FV \bullet (1 + \frac{r}{n})^{-n \cdot t}$

Discounting formula: $PV = FV \bullet (1 + \frac{r}{n})^{-n \cdot t}$

Formula Key:

FV = Future Value
PV = Present Value
r = Interest rate
n = Reinvestments per period
t = Periods of investment

Example: Suppose you are investing in a savings account with an interest rate of 7%, and annual compounding. How much will you need to invest to have $6000 after 4 years?

- From the discounting formula: $PV = 6000 \bullet (1.07)^{-4} = 4577$

66

Note: When moving money forward in time, we use the positive exponent $n \cdot t$, while when moving money back in time, we use the negative exponent $-n \cdot t$

The rate used to calculate present value is sometimes called the **discount rate** rather than the **interest rate.**

2. Your investment has future value of $2200, with a discount rate of 4%, where $t = 11$ and $n = 4$. Calculate the present value.

$$2700 \left(1 + \frac{.04}{4}\right)^{-44} = \$1419.98$$

3. Your sister wants to borrow money from you. She will graduate in three years and knows that she will receive $800 at that time. She intends to repay you with this money. You will charge 11% interest with monthly compounding. What is the most she can borrow and still pay you back with her graduation money?

$$800 \left(1 + \frac{.11}{12}\right)^{-36} = \$576.04$$

Spreadsheet Connection

It's important to calculate present value in spreadsheets too. Go through the material and questions in the worksheet 'Unit 2 Topic 5 Present Value' to learn how to do this.

Where does the discounting rate come from?

In some cases, you are told the future value of a loan or investment which comes with a certain interest rate. For example, if you take out a loan with interest rate 5% and will pay back $1000 in 4 years' time.

- In such cases, the discounting rate used to calculate present value is specified at the time of the loan.

Sometimes, you have to decide the present value of future payment, where no such interest rate is specified.

- *Example*: I offer to pay you $200 in one year if you give me $190 today.
- How do you decide whether or not to accept my offer?

In these cases, you must use your **personal discounting rate**: How much more do you value money now than at a certain point in the future?

- This is determined by how you could use the money if you had it now rather than in the future.
- For example, you could invest the money or use it to pay off a current debt.
- Note, that you don't just pick whatever personal discounting rate you want – it's determined by your financial opportunities.
- In economics, this called the **opportunity cost** of not having use of the money in the present.

Example 1: You have access to a savings account with an interest rate of 2% (and nothing better). Therefore, your discounting rate is 2%. Recall the offer to receive $200 in one year if you pay $190 today:

- Since your discounting rate is 2%, the present value of $200 in one year is $\frac{200}{1.02} =$ 196.08
- The amount you'd have to pay is less than the present value of the future payment so you should take the offer.

Example 2: You have over $1000 in credit card debt with an interest rate of 20% (and nothing with a higher rate). Therefore, your personal discounting rate is 20% because having money now allows you to avoid interest expenses accruing at a rate of 20%. Recall, again, the offer to receive $200 in one year if you pay $190 today:

- Since your discounting rate is 20%, the present value of $200 in one year is $\frac{200}{1.2} =$ 166.67
- The amount you'd have to pay is greater than the present value of the future payment so you should not take the offer.

Directions: For the following questions assume there is no further relevant information beyond what is provided.

4. You have access to a savings account with an interest rate of 3.2%. What is the present value of $800 received in one year?

68

5. You have student loan debt of $10,000 with an interest rate of 4.9%. What is the present value of $2000 received in ten years?

6. You have a savings account with an interest rate of 0.7%, investments with an interest rate of 6.2%, and $3000 of credit card debt with an interest rate of 24%. What is the present value of $390 received in seven years?

Applying the Rule of 72

The rule of 72 is also relevant when looking at present value: It gives you a way to estimate how many years of discounting it takes to make present value **half** of future value.

- If, for a given t, $FV = 2PV$, it follows that with that same t, $PV = \frac{FV}{2}$
- Therefore, with a discounting rate r, when $t = \frac{72}{R \cdot 100}$, $PV = \frac{FV}{2}$

Example: You have a discounting rate of 6%, which means the rule of 72 tells you that the present value of a sum of money will approximately half for every $\frac{72}{6} = 12$ years of discounting.

- This tells you that a payment of $1000 24 years from now has a present value of approximately $250.

7. You have a discounting rate of 8%. Estimate the present value of a payment of $15,000 that you will make 27 years from now.

8. Your investments are able to earn interest at a rate of 10%. You are offered a payment of $20,000 in 15 years' time. Your financial advisor tells you this has a present value of $10,000. Without using a calculator, can you tell if that advice is accurate?

Unit 2 Topic 5 Check for Understanding

Directions: Unless specifically stated otherwise, all interest should be assumed to be compounded annually.

Section 1

1. In general a dollar is worth __More__ (more/less) now than in the future.
2. The _____ the discount rate, the _____ the present value. [circle the correct answer]
   - (a.) Higher, lower
   - b. Higher, higher
   - c. Lower, lower
   - d. Cannot be determined
3. In your own words, explain what determines your personal discounting rate?

   How much you invest in the future

4. Order the following characters in terms of likely discounting rate from lowest (1) to highest (3):
   - 2 Terry, who has federal student loan debt, and few investment opportunities.
   - 1 Amy, a high school student who has access to a savings account but no other financial products.
   - 3 Rosa a tech worker, who has the chance to invest in an app that's about to become hugely popular.

Section 2

5. Given that $FV = PV \cdot (1 + r)^t$, solve for *PV*. *Reminder: That means get PV alone on one side of the equation.*

   $FV \left(\frac{1}{1+r} \right)^{-t} = PV$

6. Sophie has $8920 after investing for 4 years with an interest rate of 4.7%. How much did she initially invest?

   $8920 = PV \cdot (1 + .047)^4$ $8920 = PV \cdot (1.047)^4$

   $8920 = PV \cdot 1.2016 74172$ $PV = 7422.97

   $\dfrac{8920 = PV \cdot 1.2016 74172}{1.2016 74172}$

7. Hannah has $3000 after investing for a year with monthly compounding and an annual rate of 2%. How much did she initially invest?

$$3000 = PV \cdot (1 + .02)^{12} \qquad 3000 \cdot \left(1 + \frac{.02}{12}\right)^{12} \quad \$2940.64$$

$$PV = \$2365.43$$

Section 3

Directions: For the following questions, assume there is no further relevant information beyond what is provided.

8. Phil has access to a CD account with an interest rate of 2.5%. What is the present value of $280 received in three years?

$$280 = PV \cdot (1 + .025)^3$$

$$\frac{280}{1.025^3} = \$260.00$$

9. Jack has a bank loan for $2,000 with an interest rate of 7.9%. What is Jack's personal discounting rate? What is the present value of $2000 received in 5 years?

$$2000 = PV \cdot (1 + .079)^5$$

$$2000 \cdot (1.079)^{-5} = 1367.40$$

$$\frac{2000}{(1.079)^5}$$

10. Andy has access to a MMA account with an interest rate of 1.2%, investments with an interest rate of 11.6%, and $30000 of student loan debt with an interest rate of 5.1%. What is the present value of $11,000 received in five years?

MMA Account

$$11,000 \cdot (1.116)^{-5} \qquad \$6354.36$$

Section 4

11. You have a discounting rate of 3.6%. Estimate the present value of a payment of $401, made 40 years from now, using the rule of 72.

$$401 = \frac{72}{3.6} = 20 \quad 1443.6$$

$$400/4 = 100.25$$

12. Your investments are able to earn interest at a rate of 9%. You are offered a payment of $40,000, received 24 years from now. Your financial advisor tells you this has a present value of approximately $10,000. Without using a calculator, can you tell if that advice is accurate?

NO

~~Yes~~ or around it b/c

10% is 4000

72/M = 8

PV of payment is approximately 40000/8 = 5000, so financial advisor is wrong

Spreadsheet Connection

Now complete the questions on the document 'Unit 2 Topic 5 Check Sheet'.

TOPIC 6: EARNING INTEREST IN THE FINANCIAL LIFE CYCLE

Introducing the Financial Life Cycle

Cara is a high school senior, who is thinking about what comes next. To get some ideas about her future, she reflects on the situation of some of her family members:

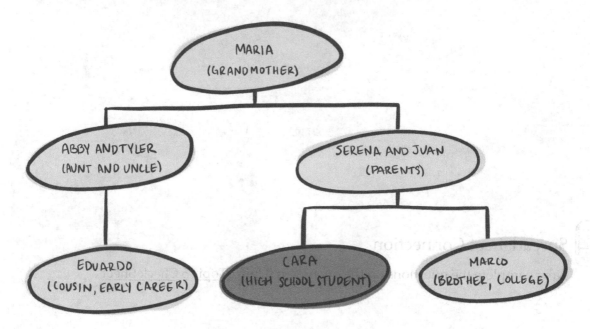

Character	Relationship	Information
Marco	Cara's older brother	• He is currently attending college, gaining a degree in economics. • He is living with his parents and working part time at a nearby coffee shop.
Eduardo	Cara's cousin	• He has just graduated college with a degree in computer science. • He has just started a job maintaining the website for a local business.
Serena and Juan	Cara's parents	• Serena works as a nurse while Juan is a high school history teacher. • They have three children, Marco and Cara, along with Cara's younger sister who is still in middle school. • Juan has been a teacher for 10 years, while Serena has been a nurse for 20 years.

Abby and Tyler	Cara's Aunt and Uncle	• Abby is a dentist and Tyler is an accountant. • They have one child, Eduardo, who is no longer living with them. • They have both been working for 25 years.
Maria	Cara's Grandmother	• She used to work in advertising, but she is now retired. • She lives alone, close to Cara and her family.

1. Read through the information on Cara's family members. Given what you've learned, write down some of the key sources of income and expenses for them (there's no single correct answer here, just think about what might be plausible for someone in their situation).

Character	Income	Expenses
Marco		
Eduardo		
Serena and Juan		
Abby and Tyler		
Maria		

2. Based on your answer to question 1 and using the table below, try to rank the income levels and the expense level of Cara's family members from lowest to highest.

Character	Marco	Eduardo	Serena & Juan	Abby & Tyler	Maria
Income Rank					
Expense Rank					

74

3. Given your answers to question 2, do you think Cara's family member's income level will always match their expense level?

Using the different members of Cara's family as a model, we can divide a person's life into various stages, which each family member being representative of a stage:

1. Education (Marco)
2. Early Career (Eduardo)
3. Family (Serena and Juan)
4. Late Career (Abby and Tyler)
5. Retirement (Maria)

4. In general, how do you expect levels of income and expense vary across these life stages?

Life Cycle Stage	Notes on Income Level	Notes on Expense Level
1. Education		
2. Early Career		
3. Family		
4. Late Career		
5. Retirement		

Unpacking the Financial Life Cycle

We can make some generalizations about the typical financial situation in the various life cycle stages, as displayed in the following graph:

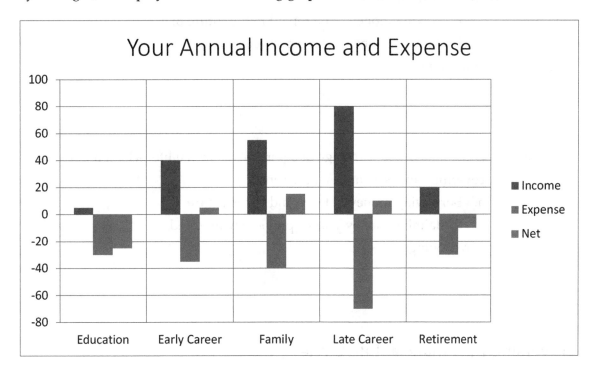

As the diagram shows, income and expense levels do not always match.

- When income is higher than expense, that's not so bad: it means you have money left over when you've covered all your expenses.
- When expenses are higher than income, though, it looks like you're in trouble. The money you take in is not enough to pay for everything you need.

When you want to spend future income now (i.e. when you want to transport your money back in time) you must *borrow* money.

- When you borrow, a financial institution gives you money now, on the condition you repay them in the future.

When you have extra income now that you don't want to spend until later on (i.e. when you want to transport your money forward in time) you must *invest* your money.

- When you invest, you give money to a financial institution now, on the condition that they will repay you in the future.

5. We saw in the bar graph above that two stages of the life cycle in which a person's expenses are usually greater than their income are (i) education; and (ii) retirement.

    i.   During the *education* stage of a person's financial life, which method of covering expenses makes more sense?

        a. Borrowing money to be repaid in the future or

        b. Reclaiming money you've previously invested

Explain your reasoning:

    ii.   During the *retirement* stage of a person's financial life, which method of covering expenses makes more sense?

        a. Borrowing money to be repaid in the future

        b. Reclaiming money you've previously invested

Explain your reasoning:

Traversing the Financial Life Cycle

Let's combine what we've learned about the mathematics of compounding with the concept of the financial life cycle. To do this, we will examine the Financial Life Cycle through four different cases to see the effect of transferring consumption from one phase of life to another.

Example 1: The chart below shows Maria's income and expenses in her late career and her retirement.

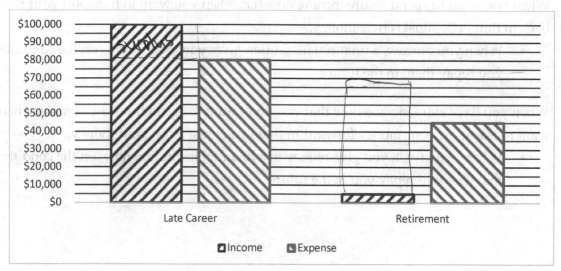

6. How much late-career surplus income does Maria have available to invest for retirement (this is the amount her income exceeds her expenses)?

    20,000

7. Maria's late-career and her retirement are 10 years apart and her investments earn 8% interest. What is the future value of her available late-career income?

    $20000 (1 + .08)^{10}$

    $43178.

8. Indicate on the graph above how Maria's financial situation is affected by the investment.
    -   Cross out the portions of bar representing income being invested from the late-career income column.
    -   Add to the bar representing income in retirement to reflect the money available to her in retirement as a result of her investment.

9. Assuming Maria saves money as you have calculated, will she have enough money to cover her expenses during retirement?

    Yes. $68178

Example 2: The graph below shows Eduardo's income and expense levels for education, early career and household phases of his life cycle.

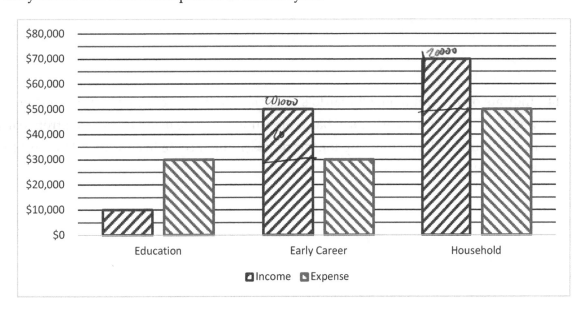

78

10. How much does Eduardo need to borrow to cover his education expenses, given his education income level?

$ 20000

11. How much does Eduardo have available to repay education loans at both early career and household phases? (List each separately)

Early Career $20,000

Household : $20,000

12. Assume each life cycle phase is 10 years apart from the next and that Eduardo's student loans have a 5% interest rate. What is the <u>present value</u> of Eduardo's surplus early career income if Eduardo transfers it to the education stage?

$20000 (1.05)^{10}

= 32577.89

13. How much of Eduardo's surplus household-phase income is required to completely meet his education expenses, assuming all his surplus early-career income, the amount you calculated in the last question, also goes towards this?

14. Indicate on the graph how Eduardo's financial situation is affected by this transfer of wealth. Cross out the portions of bar representing income being transferred from early career/household, and build up the bar representing income in education to reflect this transfer of wealth.

Example 3: The graph below shows Serena and Juan's (combined) income and expenses from all stages of their life cycle.

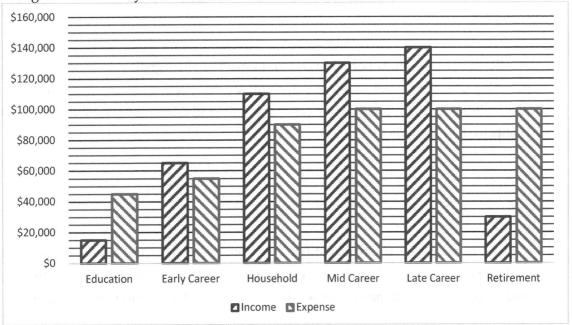

Income Expense

15. For each life cycle stage, state whether Serena and Juan have an income surplus or deficit (not enough income to cover expenses), and write down its value:

Education	Early Career	Household	Mid Career	Late Career	Retirement

16. Assume that each stage is 10 years apart and that both investments and loans have a 7.2% interest rate. Serena and Juan use their early career and household surplus to cover their education expenses – what is the present value of these sums?

17. Sketch on the graph how their financial situation is affected by these transfers. Cross out the income being transferred from early career and household and represent it as new income in the education column.

18. Serena and Juan use their mid-career and late-career surplus to cover their retirement expenses – what is the future value of these sums?

19. Sketch on the graph how their financial situation is affected by these transfers. Cross out the income being transferred to a different stage of life and represent it as new income in the appropriate columns.

20. Do these transfers allow Serena and Juan to meet all their goals and cover all of their expenses over their financial life cycle? If not, do you have any suggestions for how they could alter their plans so that they can meet their goals and cover all their expenses at all points in their financial life cycle?

21. Donald is confused. After calculating the surplus/deficit of each state of life in part a, he added them all up and found that they sum to zero. He reasons that this means Serena and Juan can cover all their expenses dollar for dollar. Explain the fault in his reasoning.

Example 4: The graph below shows Abby and Tyler's (combined) income and expenses from all stages of their life cycle.

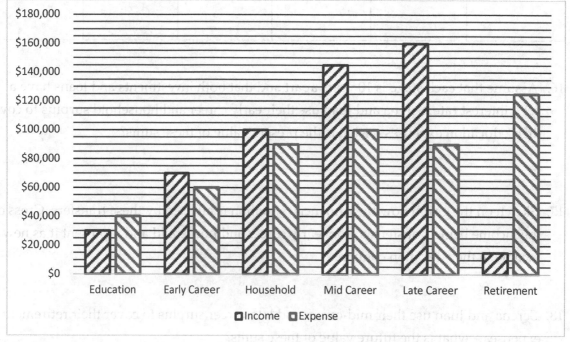

22. For each life cycle state, state whether Abby and Tyler have an income surplus or deficit and write down its value.

Education	Early Career	Household	Mid Career	Late Career	Retirement

23. Assume that each stage is 10 years apart and that loans have a 5% interest rate while investments have an 8% rate. Abby and Tyler want to use only 50% of their surplus income for covering education expenses, starting with early career and continuing until they are completely covered. Calculate the present value of each surplus in turn and explain at what stage the expenses will have been covered.

24. Abby and Tyler use the remainder of their income surplus to invest for retirement, what is the future value of each of these investments?

25. Sketch on the graph how their financial situation is affected by these transfers. Cross out the income being transferred to a different stage of life and represent it as new income in the appropriate columns.

82

Financial Products

When transferring consumption as we did in the last activity, you need to use different **financial products**. It's important to understand the different features of different instruments.

A **Financial Product** is a tool created by a company that allows you meet certain financial goals. Typically, these goals involve investing and borrowing.

Examples of Financial Products:
- A financial product for investing is a savings account.
- A financial product for borrowing is a student loan.

26. What are some other financial products for investing?

27. What are some other financial products for borrowing?

Different products come with different costs and benefits. Factors to consider include:
- **Interest rate**: This determines how quickly the debt or investment will grow.
- **Ease of access**: This concerns how easily you can add or take out money from your investment or loan – that is, the **liquidity** the product provides.
- **Risk:** This is how unpredictable the future value of your investment or loan is. We will address this issue in detail in units 4 and 5.

When investing, you want a *high* interest rate, easy access, and low risk. When borrowing, you want a *low* interest rate, easy access and low risk.
- Generally, you will have to make a **tradeoff** between these goals, depending upon your particular needs.

Example: Some investment accounts limit the number of deposits and withdrawals you can make within a given period – this **reduces** ease of access.

Below are features that some financial products may offer. Which of the following features increase ease of access for investment, and which decrease it? (Circle one)

28. Online transfers available	Increases	Decreases
29. A fee is charged for withdrawals	Increases	Decreases
30. You can withdraw invested money at an ATM	Increases	Decreases
31. There is a 7-day processing time for withdrawals	Increases	Decreases

Investment Instruments

Below are the most important kinds of financial instruments for investment:

Savings Account: Offered by banks - you loan a sum of money to a bank for an unspecified period. They have a low interest rate, are low risk and give you easy, immediate access to your money.

- You can deposit money in your savings account, at any point in time, and for any amount – through an ATM, in the bank, or online.
- You can withdraw any amount you want, whenever you want – again, through an ATM, in the bank, or online.
- Sometimes there are restrictions as to how many withdrawals you can make in a given period of time.
- The money is government guaranteed up to $250,000, so you are certain to get back all of your deposits. This is because, if the bank goes out of business, the government will repay your money. This further reduces your risk.

32. Go online and find three different savings accounts. Make a note of the name, the interest rate, any significant features that improve access, and any significant features that reduce access.

Hint: If you don't know where to start looking, you can use a site like www.bankrate.com that compares different financial products. (A full list of comparison sites is found on the research information sheet at the front of this workbook.)

Account Name	Interest Rate	Improve Access	Reduce Access

CD Account (Certificate of Deposit Account): Investment instrument provided by a bank. You loan the bank a sum of money for a fixed period (for example 5 years) and there is a fee for withdrawing the money early. In return, there is typically a higher interest rate than for a savings account.

- The money is government guaranteed, so you are sure to get back all of your deposit after the allotted time.
- They are still relatively low interest and low risk.
- Access is less flexible than with savings accounts.

33. Go online and find three different CD accounts. Make a note of the name, the interest rate, the duration of the account, and the fees for early withdrawal.

Account Name	Interest Rate	Duration	Fees

Money Market Account (MMA): Account that pays interest based on current rates in money markets – Higher interest rate, requires minimum deposit, and can be short term.

- The **money market** is where financial instruments with high liquidity are traded – this is in contrast with the **capital market**, where longer term assets are traded.
- When you have an MMA, your money is invested in the money market, and you receive interest payments from the market.
- There is a limit on how many withdrawals you can make in a month – so an MMA falls in between a savings account and a CD account in terms of ease of access.
- In general, MMA have a slightly higher interest rate than a savings account.

34. Go online and find three different MMA's. Make a note of the name, the interest rate, any significant features that improve access, and any significant features that reduce access.

Account Name	Interest Rate	Improve Access	Reduce Access

The other two most important investment products are **stocks** and **bonds** – we will explore these primarily in unit 5.

- With stocks you buy part ownership of a company and share in its profits.
- With bonds, you lend money to the government, and receive interest payments.

35. Which accounts possess the following features? (It may be more, or less, than one.)

	Savings Account	CD Account	MMA
A fixed time-period for your investment			
Immediate withdrawals			
Rolling deposits			
Interest rate linked to money markets			
Online access			
Double your money in one-year guarantee			

86

Directions: Use www.bankrate.com, or another comparison site to answer the following questions.

36. You have $3100 to invest for five years. Pick a savings account, a CD account, and a MMA that you found in your research. For each of these, calculate the future value of your investment if you put your money in that account.

37. You are trying to decide where to invest your $3100. You want to keep $1000 on hand for emergencies, but you do not plan on touching the rest over the 5 years. Based on this, what is the best way to invest your money? (You can split it across multiple accounts). Explain your answer.

38. Calculate the value of your money after five years if you invest in this way.

Borrowing Instruments

Here are some of the most important tools for borrowing:

A **Bank Loan** is when a bank lends you an agreed upon sum of money, usually with an agreed upon interest rate, and provides an agreed upon schedule for paying it back.

You can get bank loans for a range of reasons:
- Personal loan
- Business loan
- Mortgage (a loan for buying a house)

A **Student Loan** is when a bank or the government lends you an agreed upon sum of money for the explicit purpose of covering the costs of college. It is similar to a bank loan.
- This includes the cost of tuition and living expenses while you are studying.
- Government student loans are typically a little different than Bank loans:
  - Government loans typically have a lower interest rate than regular commercial rates.
  - You generally will not be required to start paying back the loan until you finish college.

As of April 2nd, 2020, the interest rate for a federal loan was **4.53%**.
- You can find out more information here
  https://studentaid.ed.gov/sa/types/loans/interest-rates

39. You take out $15,000 in federal student loans. You graduate college in 2010, but don't make any payments (not even interest payments) until 2017. How much do you owe at this point? *(Use the interest rate for a federal loan listed above.)*

Some information on private student loans can be found on financial comparison sites, such as those on the Research Sheet.

40. Find a student loan and write down its name and rate (if the rate varies, calculate the median value).

      Name of Student Loan:

      Rate:

41. Suppose you take out $15,000 with your chosen loan. How much will you owe 7 years after you graduate if you don't make any payments?

42. Now suppose you take out $10,000 in federal loans and $5000 in the private loan of your choice. How much will you owe 7 years after you graduate if you don't make any payments?

 A **Credit Card** is a tool, provided by banks, which allows you to borrow money on demand by making purchases with the card.

- You can make purchases with it as you would with a debit card, but the expenses increase your liabilities rather than reducing your cash balance.
- There is a preapproved monthly limit to how much you can borrow at any given time.

Example: A Bank of Iowa credit card has a credit limit of $99 – this means you can purchase $99 worth of goods at one time before you run out of credit.

- If you spend $60 on pizza for all your friends your balance will be $60 and you have $99 – 60 = $39 left to spend with your card.
- If you then go online and make a $25 payment from your checking account towards your balance (meaning you give the Credit Card company $25), your new balance will be $60 – 25= $35 and you have $99 –35 = $64 left to spend on your card.

43. You get a credit card from the Bank of Wyoming with a credit limit of $163.
    - You spend $96 on videogames, then pay $38 towards your balance.
    - What is your current balance and your current available credit?

Interest rates on credit card debt is usually very high and can be over 25%.

The interest rate for credit cards is often referred to as **APR** which stands for **Annual Percentage Rate**.

44. *Krazy Kredit Kard* has an interest rate of 23%: you use it to buy an $800 TV. You then do nothing for 2 years. What is your balance at this point?

45. Using the rule of 72, estimate how long it takes for debt on *Krazy Kredit Kard* to double.

There are some other key features to keep in mind when looking at credit cards:

Promotional Rates: Credit cards often have promotional rates that offer more favorable interest rates when you first get the card.
   - *Example*: *Krazy Kredit Kard* charges 0.8% interest for the first 6 months you own the card and afterward charges 23%.

Grace Period: Credit cards often come with a 'grace period', which means that if you pay back money soon after you borrow it, you will not be charged any interest (Typically the grace period is one month).

Cash Back: Credit cards often come with rewards for making certain purchases. The most common reward is **cash back** which means that when you spend a certain amount, you get a percentage of that amount refunded on your card – so with 1% cash back, for every $100 you spend, you get $1 taken off your balance.

90

46. Which of the following is most likely to be an interest rate for a credit card?

    a. 2%

    b. 7%

    c. 27%

    d. 90%

47. The length of time after a purchase in which you are not charged interest is known as a
_____ period.

48. If a credit card offers a "promotional rate" that means when you initially get the credit card, the interest rate will be _____ (higher / lower) than it will be when the promotional period ends.

49. You have a credit card with 1% cash back. If you pay $20 in interest expenses one month, how much would you have to spend on the card to earn $20 via cashback, and make up for the interest expense? Given your answer, do you think earning cash back is an effective way to counterbalance credit card fees?

Directions: Research information about credit cards online on your favorite comparison site.

50. Pick three cards and note the key details: APR, grace period, promotional rate, cash back, any other fees or offers.

Card Name	APR	Grace Period	Promotional Rate	Cash Back	Other Comments

Credit Card Tips:

The rule of 72 tells you that, with interest rates over 20%, interest on credit card debt gets very large, very quickly.

- However, with a monthly grace period, if you use your credit card but pay off your purchases, reducing the balance to zero at least once a month, you will never be charged any interest.
- If you do this, you will earn cashback, effectively reducing overall expenses.
- You can ensure you stick to the plan by ensuring that the amount you owe on the card is never more than your cash savings (while also accounting for upcoming expenses).
- Making such use of a credit card also improves your credit score which is something we will discuss in topic 7.

51. Describe a situation in which it would be a good idea for someone to make use of a credit card.

52. Describe a situation in which it would be a bad idea for someone to make use of a credit card.

Interest Calculations in Financial Statements

Often, we want to keep track of interest accrued via various financial instruments within our financial statements.

As we saw in unit 1, to keep complete track of our financial transaction, we need the following: a starting balance sheet, an income statement, and an ending balance sheet. However, we need to first calculate interest income and interest expenses, in order for them to be included on the income statement.

- For this, it's best to note down the variable values that go into this calculation (interest rate and compounding period) on the financial statements.

Here's an example of how to lay this out:

Starting Balance Sheet			
Assets		Liabilities	
		Credit	
Cash	7000	Card	900
		Student	
Car	3000	Loans	15000
Total	10000	Total	15900
		Net Worth	(5900)

The interest table lists the key figures with regard to interest on current investments and liabilities. With this, and the values in the starting balance sheet, their future value can be calculated using the compounding formula.

Interest Table				
Liability	Rate	Compounding	Year	FV
Credit Card	28%	12	1	1186.99
Student Loans	3.76%	1	1	15564

The interest income and expenses are the differences between future value and present value for investments and liabilities respectively and are added to the income statement.

Income Statement

Income		Expenses	
		Credit Card Interest	286.99
		Student Loan Interest	564
Total	0	Total	850.99
		Net Income	(850.99)

Ending Balance Sheet

Assets		Liabilities	
Cash	7000	Credit Card	1186.99
Car	3000	Student Loans	15564
Total	10000	Total	16750.99
		Net Worth	(6750.99)

53. Fill in the gaps in the financial statements below:

Starting Balance Sheet

Assets		Liabilities	
Cash	1300	Credit Card	2300
CD Account	8000		
Total	9300	Total	2300
		Net Worth	7000

Interest Table

Investment/Liability	Rate	Compounding	Period	FV
CD Account	3.5%	Continuous	1	
Credit Card	19.5%	4	1	

94

Income Statement

Income		Expenses	
CD Interest		Credit Card Interest	
Total		Total	
		Net Income	

Ending Balance Sheet

Assets		Liabilities	
		Credit	
Cash	1300	Card	
CD Account			
Total		Total	
		Net Worth	

 Spreadsheet Connection

The most convenient option is to calculate interest in financial statements in a spreadsheet. Work through the document 'Unit 2 Topic 6 Calculating interest in financial statements' to understand this.

Unit 2 Topic 6 Check for Understanding

Section 1:

Directions: Fill in each blank using the word bank. You may need to use some of the words more than once:

[WORD BANK: student loans, mixed martial arts, high, low, money market account, savings accounts, sticker, mixed martial arts, period of time, grace period, products]

1. You can use financial _____ to transfer consumption over time.

2. With a CD account, you must commit to investing for a fixed _____.

3. In the context of finance, MMA stands for _____.

4. Savings accounts and money market accounts are similar, except _____ generally have higher interest rates.

5. The government provides _____ to help people cover the cost of college education.

6. A credit card lets you borrow money at short notice with a _____ interest rate

7. Credit cards often have a _____ during which no interest is charged on the money you owe.

Section 2:

Directions: Circle the correct answer.

8. Certificates of deposit usually have a _____ rate of return than savings accounts.
   a. Lower
   b. Higher
   c. Sometimes lower and sometimes higher
   d. Similar

9. Which of the following is NOT true about certificates of deposit?
   a. Early withdrawals are penalized
   b. CDs are usually low-risk, low-return
   c. CDs are usually high-risk, high-return
   d. CDs usually mature in short to medium time frames

10. What is the problem with investing all your money in a CD account?
   a. You could lose it if markets crash
   b. The government might be unable to pay you
   c. You will not be able to access it quickly in an emergency
   d. You should always invest in gold

Section 3:

11. Hanna has $3200 she wants to invest. She doesn't need to use it for day to day expenses, but she may need to use it if she faces unexpected costs.
    - She is deciding between investing in a savings account with an interest rate of 0.97%, a 3-year CD account with a rate of 2.1%, and an MMA with a rate of 1.8%
    - Which account would you advise Hanna to use? Explain your answer.
    - Calculate the future value after three years if she follows your advice.

12. has $60,000 saved that he wants to use as a down-payment on a house in 5 years' time. In the meantime, he wants to invest it.
    - He is deciding whether to invest is in a savings account with 1% interest, a 5 year CD account with 2.5% interest, or a high interest 10 year CD and a rate of 4.5%.
    - Which account would you advice Ian to use? Explain your answer.
    - Calculate the future value after 5 years if he follows your advice.

13. Marco is entering his senior year in college. In order to graduate on time, he will have to quit his part time job, which means he needs to find a way to replace the lost income to cover expenses.

- He can either pay for extra expenses on his credit card as necessary, or he can take out additional student loans.
- What would you advise Marco to do? Explain your answer.

14. Nina has $1000 in cash savings. She is deciding whether to use this money to invest in a CD account or pay off her credit card debt. What would you advise her to do? Explain your answer.

 Spreadsheet Connection

Now complete the questions on the document 'Unit 2 Topic 6 Check Sheet'.

TOPIC 7: CREDIT SCORES

At certain stages in the financial life cycle, you need to borrow money to transfer consumption forward.

1. The mathematics of compounding gives you theoretical tools to calculate the present value of a loan.
2. Practically speaking, you need to look at your **credit score** to know whether or not you can get a loan.

A **Credit Score** is a tool used by lenders to assess the risk that a customer will be unable to repay them on time. It is a number assigned to each individual person. A good credit score provides 3 key benefits:

a. It allows you to get credit faster.

b. It gives you a better rate of interest.

c. It gives you access to more credit (many kinds of loans require a minimum credit score to be granted at all).

The most commonly used credit score is the FICO® score. Your FICO® score is a number between 300 and 850, the higher the better – generally, scores above 720 are regarded as 'good' scores, and scores above 800 are regarded as 'very good'. This number is calculated by looking at five kinds of information:

- Payment history
    - This is your track record of making payments on time, or failing to do so.
    - A longer payment history improves your credit score, provided the payments aren't late.
- Amounts owed:
    - This is amount of money you currently owe, taking into account all the different places you owe money, and how much more credit you have available.
    - Owing lots of money to a range of sources lowers your credit score, as does approaching your credit limit.
- Length of credit history:
    - This is how long you have been making payments.
    - Starting a credit history earlier will improve your credit score in the long run, provided you are able to make payments on time.
- Credit mix:
    - the different types of credit accounts you have.

- o Having different kinds of credit available (e.g. mortgage, car loan, and credit card) improves your credit score – having many different credit cards will *not* improve your score.
- New credit:
    - o This is how much credit you recently received or requested.
    - o Applying for a lot of new credit all at once will lower your credit score.
    - o Note that this includes singing up for multiple credit cards at once.

The relative importance of each of these categories is shown by the diagram below:

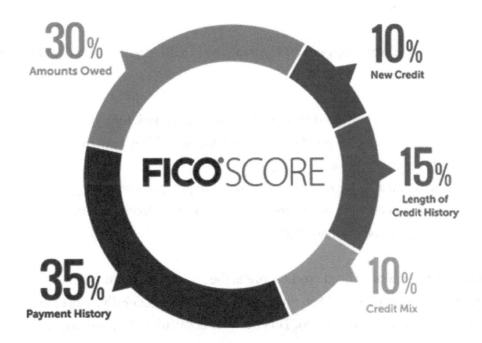

[Image source https://www.myfico.com/]

The two crucial things you can do to maintain and cultivate a good credit score are:
1. Make all payments on time – both for bills and loan repayments.
2. Keep down how much you owe – in particular, pay off any credit card debt.

Check your Knowledge on Credit Scores

Directions: Use the word bank to fill in the blanks on the credit score info sheet:

[Word Bank: in person, height, lowers, on time, raises, make payments, 1080, longer, not improve, shorter, credit score, FICO, dance, Geico, loan, 720, higher, owe, own, limit, lower]

At certain stages in the financial life cycle, you need to borrow money to transfer consumption forward.

1. The mathematics of compounding gives you theoretical tools to calculate the present value of a loan.

2. Practically speaking, you need to look at your *credit score* to ensure you can get a _____.

3. A credit score is a tool used by lenders to assess the risk that a customer will be unable to _____ on time. A good credit score provides 3 key benefits:
    a. It allows you to get a _____ faster.
    b. It gives you a better rate of credit (you can get loans at a _____ interest rate).
    c. It gives you access to more credit (many kinds of loans require a minimum _____ to be granted at all).

4. The most commonly used credit score is the _____ score. Your FICO score is a number between 300 and 850, the higher the better (generally, scores above _____ are regarded as 'good' scores). This number is calculated by looking at five kinds of information:

5. Payment history: this is your track record of making payments on time, or failing to. A _____ payment history improves your credit score, provided the payments aren't late.

6. Amounts owed: this is amount of money you currently owe.
    Owing lots of money to a range of sources _____ your credit score, as does approaching your credit _____

7. Length of credit history: this is how long you have been making payments.
    Starting a credit history earlier, provided you are in a position to make payments on time, will improve your credit score in the long run.

8. Credit mix: the different types of credit accounts you have.
   Having different kinds of credit available (e.g. mortgage, car loan, and credit card)
   _____ your credit score – having many different credit cards will _____ your
   score.

9. New credit: this is how much credit you received or requested recently.
   Applying for a lot of new credit all of a sudden will _____ your credit score.

10. The two crucial things you can do to maintain a good credit score are:
    Make all payments _____ – both for bills and loan repayments.
    Keep down how much you _____ – in particular, pay off any credit card debt.

Try it out: You can check your own credit score online at sites like creditkarma.com

- You will need a social security number and valid ID.

Unit 2 Topic 7 Check for Understanding

1. What is a credit report? Explain

2. FICO scores range from:
   a. 300 to 850
   b. 600 to 700
   c. 400 to 700
   d. 300 to 800

3. Which of the following does a good credit score NOT provide?
   a. A better rate of credit
   b. Access to credit faster
   c. Access to more kinds of credit
   d. Access to loans that you do not have to repay

4. Explain why a landlord might be interested in a potential tenant's credit score.

5. For each of the following, decide how the action in the left column affects your credit score. Circle the correct option in the right-hand column:

Paying your credit card balance off at the end of each month	Increase / Decrease / No Effect
Being late on a utilities payment	Increase / Decrease / No Effect
Wearing a nice suit	Increase / Decrease / No Effect
Maintaining a line of credit for a long period of time	Increase / Decrease / No Effect
Opening 10 credit cards all at once	Increase / Decrease / No Effect
Taking out a mortgage	Increase / Decrease / No Effect
Approaching your credit limit	Increase / Decrease / No Effect
Keeping a lot of cash in your wallet at all times	Increase / Decrease / No Effect
Having a large amount of credit available	Increase / Decrease / No Effect
Writing checks rather than using a debit card	Increase / Decrease / No Effect

Unit Summary

This unit explains the effects of transferring consumption over time.

- You must pay to accelerate consumption, and you will be paid to transfer consumption to the future.
- Value increases exponentially over time, due to **compounding.**

When looking to invest or borrow, there are three key factors you need to consider.

- Interest rate
- Ease of access (or flexibility)
- Risk

To get more favorable loans, you must have a good **credit score.**

Here are the most important formulae from Unit 2:

Compound interest formula:
$$FV = PV \cdot (1 + \frac{r}{n})^{n \cdot t}$$

Continuous compounding formula:
$$FV = PV \cdot e^{rt}$$

Discounting formula:
$$PV = FV \cdot (1 + \frac{r}{n})^{-n \cdot t}$$

Simple Compounding to Continuous Compounding:
$$PV \cdot e^{rt} = PV \cdot (1 + R)^t, r = \ln(1 + R)$$

Rule of 72:
$$t = \frac{72}{R \cdot 100}$$

Formula Key:

FV = Future Value
PV = Present Value
r = Interest rate
n = Reinvestments per period
t = Periods of investment
R = Equivalent interest rate with simple compounding

Mathematics Content Review: To master the financial content in this unit, you must understand the concepts and procedures associated with, and be able to complete the worksheets related to:

- Logarithms Worksheet (found in Topic 4)
- Exponents Rules Worksheet (found in Topic 2)

GLOSSARY

APR: Stands for 'Annual percentage rate' – it is a government regulated measure of annual interest rate. It takes the interest payments over a year, including any fees and compounding, and gives the equivalent as a *simple* annual interest rate.

Bank Loan: When a bank lends you an agreed upon sum of money, usually with an agreed upon interest rate, and provides an agreed upon schedule for paying it back

Bonds: Financial product issued in return for a loan to a government or institution. Owning a bond entitles you to periodic payments, as well as full repayment when the loan ends (this is called maturity).

Borrowing: When you transfer money backwards from your future self

Cash Back: A common type of credit card reward in which you get a percentage of your spending amount refunded on your card

CD Account: Investment instrument provided by a bank. You loan the bank a sum of money for a fixed period (for example 5 years) and there is a fee for withdrawing the money early. In return, there is typically a higher interest rate than for a savings account.

Compounding: When you earn interest on the interest earned in previous periods.

Compounding formula: $FV = PV \cdot (1 + r)^t$

Compound interest: When interest is compounded, you take your interest, and reinvest multiple times during the period in order to earn interest on your interest. The formula for compound interest is $FV = PV \cdot (1 + \frac{r}{n})^n$, where n is the number of times you reinvest during the period.

Continuous compounding: This is when one takes the limit of what can be earned through compounding. That is $FV = \lim_{n \to \infty} PV \left(1 + \frac{r}{n}\right)^n$. Equivalently $FV = e^{rt}$

Continuous compounding formula: $FV = e^{rt}$

Credit Score: A tool used by lenders to assess the risk that a customer will be unable to repay them on time

Discounting: The process of calculating the present value of a given sum paid in the future

Discount Rate: The rate used to calculate present value – an alternative term for **interest rate**.

Exponential Growth: When a value increases by multiplying by a constant ratio each period

Financial Product: A tool created by a company that allows you to meet certain financial goals, typically investing and borrowing

Future value (FV): The value a given sum of money will be worth at a certain point in the future.

Grace Period: Time period within which you are not charged interest on credit card balance (typically one month).

Interest: The additional value that money invested or borrowed acquires over time.

Interest rate (r): Percentage rate that determines the value of interest added after each period.

Investing: When you transfer money forward to your future self

Investments: Money transferred to the future by means of a financial product.

Linear Growth: When a value increases by adding a constant amount each period

Loan: Money transferred to the present from the future by means of a financial product

Money market account (MMA): Account that pays interest based on current rates in money markets.

Present value (PV): The value now of a sum of money that will be received or paid at some point in the future.

Principal: The initial amount of money deposited or invested.

Promotional Rates: More favorable interest rates that apply for a limited time when you first get a credit card.

Return: The amount received from an investment.

Savings Account: Investment tool offered by banks. You loan a sum of money to a bank for an unspecified period): they have a low interest rate, are low risk, and give you easy (almost) immediate access to money.

Simple interest: When interest payments are made only on the principal, not on previously earned interest.

Simple interest formula: $FV = PV \cdot (1 + rt)$

Student Loan: A bank or the government lends you an agreed upon sum of money for the explicit purpose of covering the costs of college

Time-value of money: The changing value of a sum of money at different points in time. The value of an investment is generally expected to grow over time.

UNIT 3: REGULAR PAYMENTS

INTRODUCTORY MATERIAL

Looking Ahead

Previous units discuss transactions in which we invest or borrow a given amount of money at one point in time and reclaim or repay it in full at a later time. Often, though, we receive returns or make repayments in *installments*. For example: we usually make monthly payments on a mortgage. When we have regular payments, calculating interest becomes more complex. We face questions like the following: if you borrow $5000 with 8% APR, and make payments of $200 per month, how long will it take you to pay the loan off? To answer these questions, we need to calculate *series*.

Learning Objectives

After completing this unit, students will be able to:

- Understand concepts related to constant payments and growing cash flows
- Work with arithmetic and geometric series
- Use series to calculate mortgage payments
- Understand how inflation affects the value of a cash flow
- Use limits to calculate the value of perpetuities

TOPIC 1: ARITHMETIC SERIES

Your brother lends you $1000 with 10% APR, and he requires that you pay him back within two years.

1. If you make a single lump sum payment at the end of two years – how much will you have to pay?

2. Now suppose you pay in two installments: $600 after the first year, and the rest after the second year. How much do you pay in total?
    Hint: Make sure you first calculate the amount owed after one year, then subtract the first payment, then calculate interest earned over the second year.

3. In general, if you have to pay back a loan within a certain time frame, will you pay more if you pay in installments, or all at the end? Why? Explain you answer. If you're struggling to answer, use your answers from #1 and #2 to help you generalize.

4. Suppose you want to pay off the loan in two *equal* installments (one at the end of each year). What will be the value of each installment?
    Hint: This requires some good honest algebra.
    - Let a stand for the value of the annual payments.
    - Since the two payments together pay off the loan completely, we know the present value for the two payments is 1000.
    - That is, $1000 = a \cdot 1.1^{-1} + a \cdot 1.1^{-2}$
    - $(a \cdot 1.1^{-1})$ represents the present value of your first payment.
    - $(a \cdot 1.1^{-2})$ represents the present value of your second payment.

- Now if you find a, you have the answer.

5. Now you take out a $100,000 loan that you must pay back within 20 years. Again, you want to pay it off in 20 annual payments of equal value. Can you calculate the value of each payment?

   Hint: The answer is most likely *no, not yet* – though you should play around to see how far you can get. To answer this with a manageable calculation, we need to use some new math.

In Unit 2 we've focused on transactions in which we invest or borrow a given amount of money at one point in time and reclaim or repay it in full at a later time.

- Often, though, we receive returns or make repayments in multiple *installments*.
- For example: we usually make monthly payments on a mortgage
- Investors will often receive regular returns on their investments called *dividends*.

When we have regular payments, calculating interest becomes more complex. We face questions like the following:

- If you borrow $5000 with an 8% interest rate, and make payments of $200 per month, how long will it take you to pay the loan off?
- Suppose you will receive payments of $50 per week for 5 years. With a discounting rate of 5%, what is the present value of all these payments?
- You want to have $50,000 saved in 10 years' time. With an interest rate of 6%, how much will you have to invest per month to achieve this goal?

To answer these questions, we need to calculate *series*. To do that we first need to discuss sequences.

Arithmetic Sequences

An **Arithmetic Sequence** is a sequence of numbers, which increases by a constant amount:

Example 1: 1 , 3 , 5 , 7 , 9

+2   +2   +2   +2

Example 2: 8 , 13 , 18 , 23 , 28

+5   +5   +5   +5

6. Write down the next 3 terms for the sequence from example 2.

   8 , 13 , 18 , 23 , 28, ___ , ___ , ___ , ...

The **common difference** is the constant amount by which the terms increase.

- In order for a sequence to be arithmetic this difference cannot change.

The place a term occurs in the sequence is its **index** or **term number.**

- In the sequence 2, 4, 6 the index for 2 is 1, the index for 4 is 2 and the index for 6 is 3

We often refer to the *n*th term in an arithmetic sequence using the expression a_n

- So a_1 means the first term in the sequence, a_3 means the third term in the sequence etc.

Example: In the sequence 1, 3, 5, 7, 9,... the common difference is 2, $a_1 = 1$, $a_3 = 5$, the index for 9 is 5.

Given the sequence: 1, 6, 11, 16, ,21, 26, ...

7. What is the common difference?
8. What is a_1?
9. What is a_5?
10. What is the index for 16?

Note: Both the first term and the common difference may be negative, a decimal or a fraction.

- The arithmetic sequence that begins 8, 6, 4,... has a common difference of -2
- The arithmetic sequence 1.1, 1.6, 2.1,... has a first term of 1.1 and a common difference of 0.5

11. Write the next three terms for the arithmetic sequence that begins -1, -11, -21...

12. Write the first five terms of the arithmetic sequence where $a_1 = 3.7$ and the common difference is 0.02

We can further understand arithmetic sequences if we stack the terms vertically, in a table, rather than horizontally.

Example:

Index	Value
1	1
2	3
3	5
4	7
5	9

- The right-hand column lists the arithmetic sequence, starting at the top and going down.
- The left-hand column tells us the place in the sequence of each value.
- We can see from the table to the left that 7 is the fourth term in the sequence.

13. Put the given sequence into the given table:

1, 6, 11, 16, 21, 26, ….

Index	Value

Calculating Arithmetic Sequences

How do we calculate the terms in an arithmetic sequence?
- We can find the next term by using the previous term.
- To find the next value in the table, look at the value in the row above, and add the common difference to it.

This is known as a **recursive definition** or **recursive formula** – a definition of a sequence that tells you how to get the next term by performing an operation on the previous term.

The **Recursive Formula** for arithmetic sequences: $a_{n+1} = a_n + d$

Formula Key:
a_n refers to the nth term in the sequence
d is the common difference.

---

14. What is the recursive definition used to get the next term in the following arithmetic sequence? 7, 11, 15, 19…

What if you know the first term and common difference, but want to work out the 100th term of an arithmetic sequence?

- To find this out using the recursive definition would require going through all 100 terms of the sequence, which is a rather time-consuming process.
- Instead, we can calculate a given term using the first term, the common difference, and its **index**.

Index	Value	Value rewrite #1	Value rewrite #2
1	1	1	1
2	3	1 + 2	1 + 1*2
3	5	1 + 2 + 2	1 + 2*2
4	7	1 + 2 + 2 + 2	1 + 3*2
5	9	1 + 2 + 2 + 2	1 + 4*2

Note that each term is equal to the sum of the first term and the common differences repeatedly added a number of times.

- To get all the terms of the sequence, you keep adding the common difference to the first term.
- To get the second term, you add the common difference once; to get the third term you add the common difference twice; to get the nth term, you add the common difference n-1 times.

Symbolically: $a_n = a_1 + (n - 1) * d$

- This is known as the **explicit formula** for an arithmetic sequence.

An **explicit formula** for a sequence allows you to calculate the value of a term in a sequence, as a function of its index, without making reference to previous terms in the sequence.

15. What is the 20th term of the arithmetic sequence with first term 11 and common difference 4?

16. What is the 55th term of the arithmetic sequence that begins 56, 58, 60….?

17. What is the nth term of the arithmetic sequence that begins -10, -3, 4….?

Spreadsheet Connection

Arithmetic sequences are well-suited to being created in a spreadsheet. Work through 'Unit 2 Topic 1 Series in Spreadsheets', to learn how to do this.

Arithmetic Series

We are often interested in adding together the terms in an arithmetic sequence.

The sum of an arithmetic sequence is called an **arithmetic series**.

Example: For the sequence 1, 3, 5, 7, the corresponding arithmetic series is 1+3+5+7 = 16

18. What is the arithmetic series corresponding to the sequence 10, 13, 16, 19, 21?

Example: Johann Carl Friedrich Gauss grew up to be a groundbreaking mathematician. Even at a young age he was talented. At age 9, Gauss' schoolteacher, wanting a break from teaching, asked the students to sum the integers from 1 to 100, thinking it would take them the whole lesson. After a few seconds, the teacher saw Gauss sitting idle. When asked why he was not frantically doing addition, Gauss quickly replied that the sum was 5050. His classmates and teacher were astonished, and Gauss ended up being the only pupil to calculate the correct answer.
Source of story: https://brilliant.org/wiki/gauss-the-prince-of-mathematics/

Gauss discovered that there's a shortcut when calculating an arithmetic sequence: add the first and last terms, multiply by the number of terms, and divide by two.

- For the sequence 1, 2, 3, …, 100 there are 100 terms in total, so the series is equal to (100+1)*100/2 = 5050

Why does this work?
- We can see by taking an arithmetic sequence and grouping it in pairs: first the outermost pair, then the pair second from the outside, then the pair third from the outside… until we work our way to the middle.

Example: Take the sequence 1, 3, 5, 7, 9, 11; we arrange this in pairs as follows:
- 1, 11
- 3, 9
- 5, 7

We can see that the sum of each of these pairs has the same value! It is equal to the sum of the first term and the last term:
- The sum of the first pair just is the first term added to the last term: $1 + 11$
- With the second pair, the smaller term is the common difference added to the first term, while the bigger term is the common difference subtracted from the last term, which cancels out: $3 + 9 = (1+2) + (11 - 2) = 1 + 11 + (2 - 2) = 1 + 11$
- For the next pair, the process repeats itself: $5 + 7 = (3+2) + (9 - 2) = 3 + 9 + (2 - 2) = 3 + 9$ $= 1 + 11$

Therefore, to find the sum of the sequence, we need to multiply the sum of the first term and the last term by the last term:
- How many pairs are there? There must be half as many pairs as there are total terms in the sequence.
- In our example, a sequence with 6 terms gave us 3 pairs, so the series is equal to (1+11)*3 = 33

Simple Arithmetic Series Shortcut: $a_1 + a_2 + a_3 + \cdots + a_n = (a_1 + a_n) * \frac{n}{2}$

Note: What happens if there are an odd number of terms in the sequence? Then when we group it in pairs, we will have on term left over in the middle: for the sequence 1, 3, 5, 7, 9 the left-over term is five.
- This term is half the sum of the first and last term since it is exactly halfway between the two – in other words it counts as half a pair.
- The sequence has two full pairs and one half pair so its value is $2.5 * (1 + 9) = 25$

116

- For a sequence with n pairs, where n is odd, it will have $\frac{n-1}{2}$ full pairs and one half pair, so the total number of pairs is $\frac{n-1}{2} + \frac{1}{2} = \frac{n-1+1}{2} = \frac{n}{2}$
- Therefore, our shortcut still works!

Using the simple arithmetic series formula, find the sum the following arithmetic sequences:

19. 7, 10, 13, 16, 19, 22

20. 3, 13, 23, ... 93

We can simplify the formula further by using what we know about how to calculate terms in an arithmetic sequence: $a_n = a_1 + (n-1) * d$

For an arithmetic sequence with n terms, first term a_1 and common difference d, the series is equal to

$$(a_1 + a_n) \cdot \frac{n}{2} = (a_1 + [a_1 + (n-1) \cdot d]) \cdot \frac{n}{2}$$

$$= (2a_1 + (n-1) \cdot d) \cdot \frac{n}{2}$$

$$= (a_1 + \frac{(n-1) \cdot d}{2}) \cdot n$$

Example: Consider an arithmetic sequence with first term 8, common difference 6, and 23 terms:

- The corresponding series is equal to $\left(a_1 + \frac{(n-1) \cdot d}{2}\right) \cdot n = \left(8 + \frac{(23-1) \cdot 6}{2}\right) \cdot 23 = 1702$

21. Calculate the sum of the arithmetic series with first term 56, common difference 4, and 11 terms.

22. Explain in your own words how to solve Gauss' problem, without just plugging it into the arithmetic series formula.

We can express arithmetic series using sigma notation.

Math Check: Sigma Notation

Sigma Notation: 'Σ' means sum. When you have $\sum_{t=1}^{n}$ followed by a formula containing t, you take the sequence obtained by substituting numbers 1 to n for t, and add them together.

- 'Σ' is a letter in the Greek alphabet, pronounced 'sigma', which is why we call this 'sigma notation'.

Example 1: $\sum_{t=1}^{10} t = 1 + 2 + 3 + 4 + 5 + 6 + 7 + 8 + 9 + 10 = 55$

Example 2: $\sum_{t=1}^{7} 3t + 2 = (3 \cdot 1 + 2) + (3 \cdot 2 + 2) + \cdots + (3 \cdot 6 + 2) + (3 \cdot 7 + 2) = 98$

Compete the table below:

Sigma Notation	Expanded Sum	Sum
23. $\sum_{t=1}^{4} t$	1+2+3+4	10
24. $\sum_{t=1}^{5} t + 3$		
25. $\sum_{t=1}^{3} 3t - 2$		
26.	$4 + 8 + 12 + 16 + 20 + 24 + 28$	
27.	$3 + 7 + 11 + 15$	

Example 3: Take the arithmetic sequence with first term 8, common difference 6, and 23 terms.

- We know that $a_n = 8 + (23 - 1) \cdot 6$
- The series is the sum of these terms, which we express in sigma notation as:
  $\sum_{t=1}^{23} 8 + (t - 1) \cdot 6$

118

In general, for an arithmetic series with first term a, common difference d, and n terms, we can express it in sigma notation as follows: $\sum_{t=1}^{n} a + (t-1) \cdot d$

28. Express the arithmetic series with first term 56, common difference 4, and 11 terms in sigma notation.

Indices: The numbers that t takes the values of for each element the series are the **indices** of the series. For $\sum_{t=1}^{n} t$, the indices are the numbers 1-n.

- In the examples we've seen, the indices have started with 1, but that doesn't always have to be the case – the first value can be any number.

Example 1: $\sum_{t=4}^{7} t = 4 + 5 + 6 + 7$

Example 2: $\sum_{t=0}^{3} 2t + 1 = 1 + 3 + 5 + 7$

- Even if starting to count indices from zero seems a strange, we still just substitute in values for t in exactly the same way: The first term would be calculated with t=0; the second term would be calculated with t=1; the third term woud be calculated with t=2; and so on.

Complete the table below:

	Sigma Notation	Expanded Sum	Sum
29.	$\sum_{t=10}^{15} t$		
30.	$\sum_{t=3}^{8} 3t - 2$		
31.	$\sum_{t=2}$	$6 + 9 + 12 + 15$	
32.	$\sum_{t=2}$	$10 + 25 + 40 + 55 + 70$	

Switching Indices: We can express the same series in sigma notation using different indices – we just need to make the appropriate adjustments to the expression inside the sum.

Example 1: Take the series $\sum_{t=1}^{8} 2t$ and express with indices that start at 2.

- If we start our indices at 2 and end at 9, t will be one higher than it "should be" for each term in the series, this means we need to subtract one to get the right result.
- Therefore, $\sum_{t=1}^{8} 2t = \sum_{t=2}^{9} 2(t-1)$
- Simplifying, we get: $\sum_{t=1}^{8} 2t = \sum_{t=2}^{9} 2t - 2$

Example 2: Take the series $\sum_{t=1}^{20} 5(t-1) + 7$ and express with indices that start at 0.

- In this case, t is going to be one lower than it "should be", so we will have to add one to correct this.
- Therefore, $\sum_{t=1}^{20} 5(t-1) + 7 = \sum_{t=0}^{19} 5(t-1+1) + 7 = \sum_{t=0}^{19} 5t + 7$

 Complete the following equations:

33. $\displaystyle\sum_{t=1}^{12} 3t \qquad = \quad \sum_{t=2}$

34. $\displaystyle\sum_{t=1}^{12} 3t - 7 \qquad = \quad \sum_{t=0}$

35. $\displaystyle\sum_{t=1}^{15} 3t \qquad = \quad \sum_{t=0}$

36. $\displaystyle\sum_{t=1}^{5} 7t + 5 \qquad = \quad \sum_{t=2}$

37. $\displaystyle\sum_{t=1}^{100} 0.25t + 23 \quad = \quad \sum_{t=7}$

38. $\displaystyle\sum_{t=1}^{30} \frac{7t+5}{9} \qquad = \quad \sum_{t=2}$

The Arithmetic Series Formula

We can put all this together to get the final version of the **arithmetic series formula**:

Arithmetic Series Formula: $\sum_{t=1}^{n} a + (t - 1) \cdot d = \left(a + \frac{d(n-1)}{2}\right) \cdot n$

Formula Key:

d is the **common difference**

a is the **first term**

n is the **number of terms** in the series

t is the **series variable**

Use the arithmetic series formula to find the sum of the following series:

39. The arithmetic series with first term 28, common difference 7, and 15 terms.

40. The arithmetic series with first term -3, common difference 8, and 19 terms.

41. The arithmetic series 7, 107, 207, ... , 2007.

42. Rewrite the arithmetic series formula in sigma notation using indices that being at zero by completing the equation below.

$$\sum_{t=1}^{n} a + (t - 1) \cdot d = \sum_{t=0}$$

Financial Examples

You put $1 in a jar on the first day of the month, $2 on the second day,... and $10 on the tenth day. How much money will you have in the jar after ten days?

- You need to calculate the *sum* of the sequence 1, 2, 3....10
- In other words, you must calculate $\sum_{t=1}^{10} t$
- This is an *arithmetic series* where $d = 1$ and $a = 0$, so the arithmetic series formula gives us:

$$\left(\frac{1 + 10}{2}\right) \cdot 10 = 5.5 \cdot 10 = 55$$

43. At the beginning of the year you find a coffee tin packed full of money: the first week of the year you take $10; the second week you take $20; the third week you take $30... and

so on through the entire 52 weeks of the year. How much will you have taken in total by the end of the year?

We can apply this method to financial examples that involve **simple interest**.

Simple interest example: Suppose you make deposits of $100 at the end of each year for 15 years and earn simple interest at a rate of 10% on the amount deposited. How much do you have at the end of 15 years?

- Recall that with simple interest, you do not earn interest on your interest – only on the principal amount deposited.
- Each deposit earns interest for a different number of years. Your first deposit earns interest for 14 years, your second deposit for 13 years etc.
- So after 15 years, the value of your first deposit is: $100 \bullet (1 + 0.1 \bullet 14)$
- The value of your second deposit is $100 \bullet (1 + 0.1 \bullet 13)$

Speaking generally, the math is more straight-forward if we count the payments in terms of the number of years they are earning interest, rather than the year in which they were deposited.

- If a payment is earning interest for t years, its future value is $100 \bullet (1 + 0.1 \bullet (t - 1))$
- Since the final payment earns interest for 0 years while the first payment earning interest for 14, the total future value is the sum of 15 payments, where t counts from 1 through 15.
- That is $FV = \sum_{t=1}^{15} 100 + 10(t - 1)$
- We can now apply the arithmetic sequence formula:

$$\sum_{t=1}^{15} 100 + 10(t - 1) = \left(100 + \frac{10(15 - 1)}{2}\right) \cdot 15 = 2550$$

- Therefore, after 15 years you will have $2,550

122

44. You have an investment account that earns simple interest at a rate of 3%. You deposit $425 at the end of each year for 7 years. How much do you have after 7 years?

45. You borrow $2400 per month, over a year, and your debt accrues monthly simple interest at a rate of 0.5% per month (at the end of each month). Assuming you don't make any payments, how much will you owe at the end of the year?

Unit 3 Topic 1 Check for Understanding

Section 1: Arithmetic Sequences

1. Please find the missing terms of the following the arithmetic sequences:

    a. 1, 11, ____, ____, ____, 51

    b. 35, 46, ____, 68

    c. 723, ____, ____, ____, 671

    d. 4, ____, ____, ____, -24

    e. 0.0001, ____, ____, ____, ____, ____, ____, ____, ____, 0.0082

2. Find the 100th term. For full credit give the expression for the 100th term as well as the actual number.

    a. 14, 19, 24, 29 …

    b. 56, 53, 50, 47 …

Section 2: Sigma Notation

Fill in the table below:

Sigma Notation	Expanded Sum	Sum
3. $\displaystyle\sum_{x=1}^{6} x$		
4. $\displaystyle\sum_{x=1}^{4} 2x + 1$		
5. $\displaystyle\sum_{x=0}^{3} 3x - 2$		
6.	5 + 10 + 15 + 20 + 25 + 30 + 35 + 40	

7.	$8 + 21 + 34 + 47$

8. Create alternative representations of each expression, given the new starting index:

   a. $\displaystyle\sum_{t=1}^{30} 7t \qquad = \qquad \sum_{t=2}$

   b. $\displaystyle\sum_{t=1}^{13} 4.5t - 3 \qquad = \qquad \sum_{t=0}$

   c. $\displaystyle\sum_{t=1}^{n} a + t \cdot d \qquad = \qquad \sum_{t=0}$

9. You borrow $3000 per year from your Aunt each year for 15 years. She charges 5% simple interest on each payment. How much will you owe after 15 years? First express the value in sigma notation, then calculate the sum.

 Spreadsheet Connection

Complete the questions on 'Unit 3 Topic 1 Check Sheet'.

TOPIC 2: GEOMETRIC SERIES

Geometric Sequence

A **Geometric Sequence** is a sequence of numbers, which increases or decreases with each term proportional to the next – each term is equal to the previous one multiplied by a constant.

Example 1: 1 , 2 , 4 , 8 , 16
             x2   x2   x2   x2

Example 2: 8 , 40 , 200 , 1000 , 5000
             x5   x5   x5   x5

1. Write down the next 3 terms for the sequence in example 2.

Very similar things can be said about geometric series as what we said about arithmetic series, except now we must think in terms of repeated multiplication rather than repeated addition.

The first term is called the **initial constant**.
The constant amount by which the terms are multiplied is called the **common ratio**.

- *Example*: In example 1 above, the initial constant is 1 and the common ratio is 2.

2. What are the initial constant and common ratio in example 2?

Note: Either the common ratio may be negative, a decimal or a fraction.
- The geometric sequence that begins 8, 4, 2,… has a common ratio of 1/2
- The geometric sequence that begins -3, 9, -27… has a common ratio of -3

3. Write the next three terms for the geometric sequence that begins:

    1/10, 1/100, 1/1000, _____ , _____ , _____ .

4. Write the first five terms of the arithmetic sequence where the initial constant is −1 and the common ratio is −4

We defined a geometric series using **recursive definition**: you get the next term by multiplying the previous term by the common ratio.

- The **recursive formula** for geometric sequences is $a_{n+1} = a_n \cdot R$
- Here a_n refers to the nth term in the sequence, and R is the common ratio.

As with arithmetic sequences, it's also useful to find an **explicit function** for geometric sequences.

- This allows us to calculate, e.g., the 100th term in a sequence without having to calculate the previous 99.
- Putting the geometric sequence vertically, in a table, can help us see how the sequence grows.
- The table for the sequence from example 1 is below:

Index	Value	Value rewrite	Value rewrite 2
1	1	1	$1 \cdot 2^0$
2	2	1·2	$1 \cdot 2^1$
3	4	1·2·2	$1 \cdot 2^2$
4	8	1·2·2·2	$1 \cdot 2^3$
5	16	1·2·2·2	$1 \cdot 2^4$

5. Fill in a similar table for the sequence: 8, 40, 200, 1000, 5000

Index	Value	Value rewrite	Value rewrite 2
1			
2			
3			
4			
5			

Note that each term is equal to the first term multiplied by the common ratio a certain number of times.

- To get the second term, you multiply the first term by the common ratio once; to get the third term multiply by the common ratio twice; to get the nth term, you multiply by the common ratio n-1 times.

- This gives us the explicit formula:

Explicit Formula for Geometric Sequence: $a_n = a * R^{n-1}$

Formula Key:

a_n is the nth term of the sequence

a is the first term of the sequence

R is the common ratio

6. What is the 8th term of the geometric sequence with first term 6 and common ratio 3?

7. What is the 24th term of the geometric sequence that begins 10, 11, 12.1 ….?

8. What is the nth term of the geometric sequence that begins 2, -4, 8….?

Spreadsheet Connection

Geometric sequences are well-suited to being created in a spreadsheet. Work through 'Unit 3 Topic 2 Series in Spreadsheets', sheets 1-2 to learn how to do this. We will work through the remaining tabs later in this topic.

Geometric Series

We are often interested in adding together the terms in a geometric sequence.

The sum of a geometric sequence is called a **geometric series**.

- We can use the explicit formula for a geometric sequence to express a geometric series in **sigma notation**

Example: Find series corresponding to the geometric sequence 2, 4, 8, 16, 32

- The series is equal to $2 + 4 + 8 + 16 + 32$
- In sigma notation we express this as $\sum_{t=1}^{4} 2 \cdot 2^{t-1}$

For the general geometric series with first term a, common ratio R, and n terms, we write:

- $\sum_{t=1}^{n} a \cdot R^{t-1}$

9. Express in sigma notation the geometric series with first term 6, common ratio 3, and 25 terms.

As with arithmetic series, we can express geometric series in different ways by changing the indices we use in our sigma notation.

Fill in the following table – make sure you pay attention to indices.

	Sigma Notation	Expanded Sum	First Term	Common Ratio
10.	$\displaystyle\sum_{t=1}^{6} 2 * 3^{t-1}$		2	3
11.	$\displaystyle\sum_{x=1}^{4} 4 * 10^{t-1}$			
12.		$6 + 18 + 54 + 162$		
13.	$\displaystyle\sum_{t=0}^{7} 1000 * 1.05^{t}$			
14.	$\displaystyle\sum_{t=2}^{5} 4 * 10^{t-1}$			

15. Create alternative representations of each given expression given the new starting index:

a. $\displaystyle\sum_{t=1}^{12} 3^{t}$ $=$ $\displaystyle\sum_{t=2}$

b. $\displaystyle\sum_{t=0}^{30} 250 * 1.1^{t}$ $=$ $\displaystyle\sum_{t=1}$

c. $\displaystyle\sum_{t=1}^{5} 6 * 7^{t-1}$ $=$ $\displaystyle\sum_{t=0}$

d. $\displaystyle\sum_{t=1}^{100} 40{,}000 * 1.02^t \quad = \quad \sum_{t=0}$

Spreadsheet Connection

The best way to calculate geometric series is using spreadsheets. Work through 'Unit 3 Topic 2 Series in Spreadsheets, sheets 3-6 to learn how to do this.

When looking at indices for geometric series, the two most important cases are when we start at zero and when we start at one.
- Geometric series (0): $\sum_{t=0}^{n-1} a \cdot R^t$
- Geometric series (1): $\sum_{t=1}^{n} a \cdot R^{(t-1)}$
  - We can rewrite this as $\sum_{t=1}^{n} \frac{a}{R} \cdot R^t$

Because, a and n are arbitrary constants, we can redefine them to give us simpler expressions. This gives us:
- Geometric series (0): $\sum_{t=0}^{n} a \cdot R^t$
- Geometric series (1): $\sum_{t=1}^{n} a \cdot R^t$

Note that when we redefine the terms, a and n do not necessarily refer to the first term and number of terms.

16. For geometric series (0) $\sum_{t=0}^{n} a \cdot R^t$, write down the first term, common ratio, and number of terms.

17. For geometric series (1) $\sum_{t=1}^{n} a \cdot R^t$, write down the first term, common ratio, and number of terms.

Recall, that the **Arithmetic Series Formula** gave us a shortcut to calculate the value of an arithmetic series without having to do add up the terms one by one.
- We can do the same thing for geometric series using the **Geometric Series Formula**.
- There are two different versions of the formula, depending on whether the indices start at zero or one.

Geometric Series Formula (0): $\sum_{t=0}^{n} a \cdot R^t = a(\frac{1-R^{n+1}}{1-R})$

Formula Key:

R is the **common ratio** between the terms

a is the **initial constant**

n+1 is the **number of terms** in the series

t is the **series variable**

This formula shows us how to move from a summation to a single expression.

Use the Geometric Series Formula (0) to sum the following geometric series:

18. $\sum_{t=0}^{23} 100 \cdot 1.03^t$

19. The geometric series with initial constant 6, common ratio 3 and 11 terms.

20. The series whose terms form the geometric sequence that begins 10, 11, 12.1,… and has 18 terms.

21. The series whose terms form the geometric sequence that begins 2, -4, 8, …. and has 15 terms.

Note the difference in formula when the indices begin at one.

Geometric Series Formula (1): $\sum_{i=1}^{n} a \cdot R^i = a\left(\frac{1-R^n}{\frac{1}{R}-1}\right)$

Formula Key:

R is the **common ratio** between the terms

a is the **initial constant**

n+1 is the **number of terms** in the series

t is the **series variable**

132

Extension

Deriving the **Geometric Series Formula (0)**

Where does this formula come from? To see we use an algebraic trick.

First, we define a variable S, so that $S = \sum_{t=0}^{n} a \cdot R^t$ i.e.:

$$S = \sum_{t=0}^{n} a \cdot R^t = a + a * R + a * R^2 + \cdots + a * R^n$$

Then we compare it to this summation multiplied by R:

$$S * R = \sum_{t=0}^{n} a \cdot R^t * R = a * R + a * R^2 + \cdots + a * R^n + a * R^{n+1}$$

Now, the most important step, we evaluate the difference between these two sums, $S - S*R$. Since these expressions contain the same middle terms, they cancel out:

$$S = \sum_{t=0}^{n} a \cdot R^t = a + a * R + a * R^2 + \cdots + a * R^n$$

$$- S * R = \sum_{t=0}^{n} a \cdot R^t * R = a * R + a * R^2 + \cdots + a * R^n + a * R^{n+1}$$

We are left with $a - a * R^{n+1}$; therefore:

$$S - S * R = a - a * R^{n+1}$$

Finally, we need to solve for S. We know $S - S * R = S(1 - R)$, so dividing both sides gives us:

$$S = a \left(\frac{1 - R^{n+1}}{1 - R} \right)$$

And this is the geometric series formula.

22. Find a formula that is not a summation but is equivalent to the Geometric Series (1) $\sum_{t=1}^{n} a \cdot R^t$. Show how you derived it. (*Hint*: You can use the same strategy as we used for Geometric Series (0).)

Financial Examples

Suppose you make donations to a charity: $1 the first year, $2 the second year, $4 the third year and so on until you donate $512 the tenth year. How much do you donate in total?

- This time we have to calculate the geometric series $\sum_{t=0}^{9} 2^t$
- Calculating the sum of this sequence the long way would be impractical – fortunately, we do not have to so because of the **Geometric Series Formula.**
- We can see here that a=1; R=2; and n=9, so applying the **Geometric Series Formula**

(0): $\quad \sum_{i=0}^{9} 2^i = \left(\frac{1-2^{10}}{1-2}\right) = 1023$

23. Your uncle gives you cash each Christmas: $10 the first year, $30 the second year, $90 the third year, and so on for six years. How much do you receive in total?

Note on Indices: The **Geometric Series Formula (0)** assumes we start the series with i=0. Sometimes, though, we want to start with i=1, therefore we use the **Geometric Series (1).**

Example: Suppose you make donations to a charity: $2 the first year, $4 the second year, and so on until you donate 2^{10}=$1024 the tenth year. How much do you donate in total?

- This time we have to calculate value of $\sum_{t=1}^{10} 2^t$

Therefore, in our example, $PV = \left(\frac{1-2^{10}}{\frac{1}{2}-1}\right) = 2046$

24. Your uncle gives you cash each Christmas: $30 the first year, $90 the second year, and so on for six years. How much do you receive in total? (Use **Geometric Series Formula (1)** to answer this.)

WARNING: You can see from the examples above that it can make a huge difference whether a series starts from $t = 1$ or 0. Make sure you get it right with all the examples in this unit.

134

Compounding Example: You deposit $1000 at the beginning of each year into a savings account with an interest rate of 3% for 5 years. How much money will you have after 5 years?

- A payment series like this forms a **geometric series**. To see this, consider each payment separately, and calculate its future value in isolation.
- Each deposit is earning interest for a different amount of time. The first deposit is earning interest for 5 years; the second deposit is earning interest for 4 years etc.
- In general, the nth deposit earns interest for (5 + 1 – n) years.
- Therefore, the future value of the nth deposit is $1000 \cdot 1.03^{6-n}$

Payment Number	FV Formula	FV Value
1	$1000 \cdot 1.03^5$	$1159.27
2	$1000 \cdot 1.03^4$	$1125.51
3	$1000 \cdot 1.03^3$	$1092.73
4	$1000 \cdot 1.03^2$	$1060.90
5	$1000 \cdot 1.03^1$	$1030.00

We can see this is a geometric series if we reverse the order by indexing the terms by the number of years they earn interest.

- If a payment is earning interest for *n* years, it's future value will be $1000 \cdot 1.03^n$

Years earning interest	FV Formula	FV Value	Recursive Step
1	$1000 \cdot 1.03^1$	$1030.00	-
2	$1000 \cdot 1.03^2$	$1060.90	x1.03
3	$1000 \cdot 1.03^3$	$1092.73	x1.03
4	$1000 \cdot 1.03^4$	$1125.51	x1.03
5	$1000 \cdot 1.03^5$	$1159.27	x1.03

We can also express this in sigma notation: $\sum_{i=1}^{5} 1000 \cdot 1.03^i$

25. You deposit $350 per year in an MMA with an interest rate of 4.5% - you make these deposits at the start of the year, every year for 4 years.

   a. Write the formula for the future value of the deposit earning interest for *n* years.

   b. Write the formula for the future value of the *n*th deposit.

c. Fill in the table below for this payment series:

Years earning interest	FV Formula	FV Value	Recursive Step
1			
2			
3			
4			

d. Write the geometric series (using sigma notation) that describes the future value of the payment series.

What if the payment series is over 10, 20, or 40 years? Filling out the table for the future value of each payment would be incredibly time consuming. Luckily, spreadsheet software can do the work for you.

- We'll learn how to do this in topic 3.

Another way to calculate the future value of a lengthy payment series is by applying the **Geometric Series Formula**.

Compounding Example Continued:

You deposit $1000 at the beginning of each year into a savings account with an interest rate of 3%, but this time you do it for 10 years. How much money will you have after 10 years?

- As we saw above, if a payment is earning interest for n years, it's future value will be $1000 \cdot 1.03^n$
- This means, in sigma notation: $FV = \sum_{i=1}^{10} 1000 \cdot 1.03^n$
- We have a geometric series where $a = 1000$; $R = 1.03$; $n = 10$
- Note that the series starts with $i=1$, so we need to use **Geometric Series Formula (1)**

$$\sum_{i=1}^{n} a \cdot R^i = a\left(\frac{1-R^n}{\frac{1}{R}-1}\right)$$

- This gives us: $FV = a\left(\frac{1-R^n}{\frac{1}{R}-1}\right) = 1.03 \cdot 1000 \cdot \left(\frac{1-1.03^{10}}{1-1.03}\right) = 11,808$

26. You deposit $350 per year in an MMA with an interest rate of 4.5% - you make these deposits at the beginning of the year, every year for **15** years. Calculate the future value of your payment series, using the **Geometric Series Formula (1)**.

Unit 3 Topic 2 Check for Understanding

For each of the following sequences fill in the missing terms, state the common ratio, and write the formula for a_n.

1. 2, 4, 8, 16, _____, _____	Common Ratio = $a_n =$
2. 10, 50, 250, 1250, _____, _____	Common Ratio = $a_n =$
3. 45, -225, 1125, _____, _____	Common Ratio = $a_n =$
4. 125, 100, 80, _____, _____	Common Ratio = $a_n =$
5. 5022, 1674, 558, _____, _____	Common Ratio = $a_n =$

6. Write the first five terms of the sequence with common ratio = 6 and $a_1 = 4$.

7. Write the first five terms of the sequence with common ratio = -3 and $a_1 = 5$.

Fill in the sigma notation, the missing terms, the sum, the common ratio, and the formula for t_n.

Sigma notation	Terms	Sum / Common Ratio
8. $\displaystyle\sum_{x=1}^{5} 2 \cdot 3^{x-1}$		Sum = Common Rat. =
9. $\displaystyle\sum_{x=}$	$10 + 50 + 250 + 1250$	Sum = Common Rat. =
10. $\displaystyle\sum_{x=}$	$-24 + 72 - 216 + 648$	Sum = Common Rat. =
11. $\displaystyle\sum_{x=}$	$125 + 100 + 80$	Sum = Common Rat. =
12. $\displaystyle\sum_{x=}$	$45 - 225 + 1125$	Sum = Common Rat. =
13. $\displaystyle\sum_{x=1}^{12} 256 \cdot 1.02^{x-1}$		Sum = Common Rat. =
14. $\displaystyle\sum_{x=1}^{12} 256 \cdot 0.87^{x-1}$		Sum = Common Rat. =

 Spreadsheet Connection

Complete the questions on 'Unit 3 Topic 2 Check Sheet'.

138

TOPIC 3: ANNUITIES

An **annuity** is a financial product in which a series of equal payments are made at regular intervals.

- This may be payments you make, or payments you receive.
- Depending on the situation, you may want to calculate either the present value or future value of an annuity.

Example: In the compounding example above, we wanted to calculate the *future value* of a series of equal deposits – each $1000 – in a savings account at regular intervals – at the beginning each year.

- Therefore, this was an example of an annuity.

Are these scenarios examples of an annuity, or not? Explain your answer, referencing the definition given above.

1. You win the lottery and are paid $2000 a month for 20 years.

 Yes

2. Your uncle gives you $20 every time the Knicks win a game.

NO

3. Every month your big brother makes you give him a dollar amount equal to his age in years, for five years.

 No

4. Every week you pay your niece $2 so that she will tell your mom how hard you work at school.

 Yes

Annuity Future Value

In general, if you have annual deposits of k dollars per year (made at the start of the year), for n years at interest rate r, we have:

$$FV = \sum_{t=1}^{n} c \cdot (1+r)^t$$

We can express it in a table (see the table to the right).

Payment Number	Future Value
1	$c \cdot (1+r)^n$
2	$c \cdot (1+r)^{n-1}$
3	$c \cdot (1+r)^{n-2}$
...	...
n	$c \cdot (1+r)^1$

Future Value Factor: It is sometimes useful to isolate part of the Future Value function: $(1+r)^{n+1-t}$

- This expression tells you how much one dollar at the time of payment is worth at the term of the annuity.
- This is known as the **Future Value Factor** (or 'FV Factor').
- Therefore, Future Value = Payment*FV Factor

Payment Number	Future Value Factor	Future Value
1	$(1+r)^n$	$c \cdot (1+r)^n$
2	$(1+r)^{n-1}$	$c \cdot (1+r)^{n-1}$
3	$(1+r)^{n-2}$	$c \cdot (1+r)^{n-2}$
...	...	...
n	$(1+r)^1$	$c \cdot (1+r)^1$

Example: We can apply this to our example where c=1000, r=3%, and n=5

Payment Number	Future Value Factor	Future Value
1	$1.03^5 = 1.16$	$1000 \cdot 1.16 = 1159.27$
2	$1.03^4 = 1.13$	$1000 \cdot 1.13 = 1125.51$
3	$1.03^3 = 1.09$	$1000 \cdot 1.09 = 1092.73$
4	$1.03^2 = 1.06$	$1000 \cdot 1.06 = 1060.90$
5	$1.03^1 = 1.03$	$1000 \cdot 1.03 = 1030.00$

Since the FV factor for payment 1 is approximately 1.16, $1 at the time of the first payment is worth $1.16 at the term of the annuity – so it is worth 16% more than $1 at the term of the annuity.

140

5. How much more, as a percentage, is $1 at the time of the second payment worth than $1 at the term of the annuity?

6. Consider an annuity in which you invest $3900 per year at the beginning of the year for four years with an interest rate of 8.5%. Fill in the table:

Payment Number	Future Value Factor	Future Value
1		
2		
3		
4		

So far, we've looked at annuities for which the payments are made at the **beginning** of the year. What happens if payments are made at the **end** of the year instead?

Example: You make payments of $1000 for 5 years, at the end of each year, with an interest rate of 3%.

- In this case, the first payment would only earn interest for 4 years: it would earn interest in years 2 through 5, but it would earn no interest in the first year since it wasn't made until the end of the year.
- Similarly, the second would earn interest for 3 years, while the final payment would earn no interest at all, since it had no time at all to earn interest.
- In general, a payment in year t, would earn interest for 5-t years, so $FV = 1000 \cdot (1.03)^{5-t}$
- For the whole annuity, $FV = \sum_{t=1}^{5} 1000 \cdot (1.03)^{5-t}$

We can also put this in a table:

Payment Number	Future Value Factor	Future Value
1	$1.03^4 = 1.12551$	$1000 \cdot 1.12551 = 1125.51$
2	$1.03^3 = 1.09273$	$1000 \cdot 1.09273 = 1092.73$
3	$1.03^2 = 1.0609$	$1000 \cdot 1.0609 = 1060.90$
4	$1.03^1 = 1.03$	$1000 \cdot 1.03 = 1030.00$
5	$1.03^0 = 1$	$1000 \cdot 1 = 1000.00$

More generally, for an annuity with payment c, interest rate r, and term n:

- The first payment earns interest for n−1 years, as it doesn't earn interest in the first year, but does in years 2 through n.
- Similarly, the second would earn interest for n−2 years.
- More generally, a payment in year i earns interest for n-i year, so $FV = c \cdot (1+r)^{n-t}$
- For the whole annuity, $FV = \sum_{t=1}^{n} c \cdot (1+r)^{n-t}$

Here's how to display it in a table:

Payment Number	Future Value Factor	Future Value
1	$(1+r)^{n-1}$	$c \cdot (1+r)^{n-1}$
2	$(1+r)^{n-2}$	$c \cdot (1+r)^{n-2}$
3	$(1+r)^{n-3}$	$c \cdot (1+r)^{n-3}$
...	...	...
n	$(1+r)^{0}$	$c \cdot (1+r)^{1} = c$

7. Consider an annuity in which you invest \$3900 per year, at the end of the year, for four years with an interest rate of 8.5%. Fill in the table below:

Payment Number	Future Value Factor	Future Value
1		
2		
3		
4		

Spreadsheet Connection

These tables can be made much more quickly on a spreadsheet. Go through 'Unit 3 Topic 2 Worksheet 1 FV' to learn how to do this.

Another way to calculate the future value of annuities is by applying the geometric series formula(s).

Recall that, if you have annual deposits of k dollars per year (made at the start of the year), for n years at interest rate r, we have $FV = \sum_{i=1}^{n} c \cdot (1+r)^{i}$

- This formula can be simplified using the **Geometric Series formula (1)**: $\sum_{t=1}^{n} a \cdot R^t = a\left(\dfrac{1-R^n}{\frac{1}{R}-1}\right)$

- We substitute c for a and (1+r) for R, to get $FV = \sum_{t=1}^{n} c \cdot (1+r)^{t} = c\left(\dfrac{1-(1+r)^n}{\frac{1}{(1+r)}-1}\right)$

Annuity Future Value (B): $FV = c(\frac{1-(1+r)^n}{\frac{1}{1+r}-1})$

Formula Key:

FV is the **future value** of the annuity

r is the **interest rate**

c is the **payment amount**

n is the **number of payments** in the annuity

Example: At the beginning of each year, you loan your sister $220. If you charge her 11% interest, how much will she owe you after 7 years, if she makes no payments before then?

- Since payments are made at the beginning of the year, we can use the **Annuity Future Value (B)** formula.

- $c = 220$; $r = 0.11$; $n = 7$

- Therefore, $FV = 220 \cdot \left(\frac{1-1.11^7}{\frac{1}{1.11}-1}\right) = 2390$

8. You invest $2800 at the beginning of every year for 15 years with an interest rate of 7%. How much will you have at the term of the annuity?

$$2800 \cdot \left(\frac{1-1.07^{15}}{\frac{1}{1.07}-1}\right) \approx 75,286.55$$

9. On December 1st every year (starting in 2015), you borrow $180 from your Dad so you can buy presents for your family. He charges interest at 3% on your loan. How much will you owe on Nov 30th 2020, 5 years after your first loan, if you make no payments before then? Calculate the answer using **Annuity Future Value (B)**.

$$180 \cdot \left(\frac{1-1.03^5}{\frac{1}{1.03}-1}\right) = \$984.31$$

Now let's look at annuities where payments are made at the end of the year:

- Recall that for an annuity with payment c, interest rate r, and term n, with payments made at the end of the year: $FV = \sum_{t=1}^{n} c \cdot (1+r)^{n-t}$

- To apply the geometric series formula, we need a summation of the form $\sum a \cdot R^i$

- We get this by indexing the terms by the number of years they earn interest rather than the year the payment is made, giving us $FV = \sum_{t=0}^{n-1} c \cdot (1+r)^t$

- Note the indices run from 0 to n-1 this time because the payments are made at the end of the year.

- Therefore, we must use **Geometric Series formula (0)** $\sum_{t=0}^{m} a \cdot R^t = a(\frac{1-R^{m+1}}{1-R})$

- We substitute c for a, (1+r) for R, and *n-1* for *m* to get $FV = c\left(\frac{1-(1+r)^n}{1-(1+r)}\right) = c(\frac{1-(1+r)^n}{-r})$

$$\text{Annuity Future Value (E): } FV = c\left(\frac{1-(1+r)^n}{-r}\right)$$

Formula Key:

FV is the **future value** of the annuity

r is the **interest rate**

c is the **payment amount**

n is the **number of payments** in the annuity

Note: You can remember which formula to use by noting that 'B' stands for beginning, while 'E' stands for end.

Example: At the end of each year, you loan your brother $220. If you charge him 11% interest, how much will he owe you after 7 years, if he makes no payments before then?

- Since payments are made at the end of the year, we can use the **Annuity Future Value (E)** formula.
- c=220; r=0.11; n=7
- Therefore, $FV = c\left(\frac{1-(1+r)^n}{-r}\right) = 220 \cdot \left(\frac{1-(1.11)^7}{-0.11}\right) = 2152.32$

10. You invest $2800 at the end of every year for 15 years with an interest rate of 7%. How much will you have at the term of the annuity?

$$2800 \cdot \left(\frac{1-(1.07)^{15}}{-.07}\right) = \$70361.26$$

11. Starting in 2015 – you borrow $180 from your Mom at the end of each year to fund your January cleanse. She charges interest at 3% on your loan. How much will you owe on January 1st 2020?

$$180 \cdot \left(\frac{1-(1.03)^5}{-.03}\right) = \$955.64$$

Annuity Present Value

Similar reasoning allows us to calculate the *present* value of a loan.

Example: Suppose you take out a loan with interest rate 6% and you can afford to make payments of $500 per year for 5 years. How much can you afford to borrow if payments must be made at the beginning of the year?

- Again, we begin by looking at each payment separately. We need to discount for the appropriate number of years to see its present value.
    - You do not discount the first payment at all since it is being made now
    - For the second payment, you are paying $500 in one year's time, so with 6% interest, the present value is 500/1.06
    - In general, for the nth payment: $PV = 500/(1.06)^{n-1}$
- Summing them gives us the total value of the initial loan:
- $PV = \sum_{t=1}^{5} \frac{500}{(1.06)^t} = \sum_{t=0}^{4} \frac{500}{(1.06)^t}$

We can define the **Present Value Factor (PV Factor)** as the current value of a dollar received at some point in the future.

This gives us the following table for the annuity:

Payment Number	Present Value Factor	Present Value (PV)
1	$1.06^0 = 1$	$500 \cdot 1 = 500$
2	$1.06^{-1} = 0.94$	$500 \cdot 0.943 = 471.50$
3	$1.06^{-2} = 0.89$	$500 \cdot 0.890 = 445.00$
4	$1.06^{-3} = 0.83$	$500 \cdot 0.834 = 417.00$
5	$1.06^{-4} = 0.79$	$500 \cdot 0.792 = 396.00$

Since the PV factor for payment 5 is approximately 0.79, $1 at the time of the fifth payment is worth approximately $0.79 now. If you are repaying money in 5 years' time, you will receive about 21% less as a loan now than you will have to repay.

12. How much less, as a percentage, is $1 at the time of the third payment worth, than $1 now?

Consider the general case in which there is an annuity with payment value c, discounting rate r, and term n, with payments made at the beginning of the year:

- The first payment does not need to be discounted at all since it is made now
- The second payment is made in a years' time, so it has one year of discounting.
- The nth payment has n−1 years of discounting.
- Therefore, for the nth payment, $PV = c \cdot (1 + r)^{-(n-1)}$

Payment Number	Present Value Factor	Present Value (PV)
1	$(1+r)^0$	$c \cdot (1+r)^0 = c$
2	$(1+r)^{-1}$	$c \cdot (1+r)^{-1}$
3	$(1+r)^{-2}$	$c \cdot (1+r)^{-2}$
...	...	...
n	$(1+r)^{-(n-1)}$	$c \cdot (1+r)^{-(n-1)}$

13. Express the present value of the annuity with payment value c, discounting rate r, and term n, with payments made at the beginning of the year, using sigma notation.

14. Consider an annuity in which you receive \$2500 per year, at the beginning of the year, where your discounting rate is 5.6%. Fill in the table below:

Payment Number	Present Value Factor	Present Value (PV)
1		
2		
3		
4		

For present value too, the calculation is different if payments are made at the end of the year.

Example: Return again to the case where you take out a loan with interest rate 6%, with payments of \$500 per year for 5 years, but this time with payments at the *end* of the year.

- You must apply one year of discounting to the first payment, two years' discounting to the second payment etc.
- So, for the nth payment: $PV = \dfrac{500}{(1.06)^n}$

Payment Number	Present Value Factor	Present Value (PV)
1	$1.06^{-1} = 0.943$	$500 \cdot 0.943 = 471.50$
2	$1.06^{-2} = 0.890$	$500 \cdot 0.890 = 445.00$
3	$1.06^{-3} = 0.834$	$500 \cdot 0.834 = 417.00$
4	$1.06^{-4} = 0.792$	$500 \cdot 0.792 = 396.00$
5	$1.06^{-5} = 0.747$	$500 \cdot 0.747 = 373.63$

In the general case:

Payment Number	Present Value Factor	Present Value (PV)
1	$(1+r)^{-1}$	$c \cdot (1+r)^{-1}$
2	$(1+r)^{-2}$	$c \cdot (1+r)^{-2}$
3	$(1+r)^{-3}$	$c \cdot (1+r)^{-3}$
...	...	...
n	$(1+r)^{-(n)}$	$c \cdot (1+r)^{-(n)}$

15. Express the present value of the annuity with payment value c, discounting rate r, and term n, with payments made at the end of the year, using sigma notation.

16. Consider an annuity in which you receive $2500 per year, at the end of the year, where your discounting rate is 5.6%. Fill in the table below:

Payment Number	Present Value Factor	Present Value (PV)
1		
2		
3		
4		

Spreadsheet Connection

These tables can be made much more quickly on a spreadsheet. Go through sheets 1-6 on 'Unit 3 Topic 2 Worksheet 2 PV' to learn how to do this.

As with future value, we can also calculate the present value of annuities by applying the geometric series formula(s).

Recall that for a series of payments of c dollars for n years at rate r, when payments are made at the beginning of the year:

- $PV = \sum_{i=0}^{n-1} \frac{c}{(1+r)^i}$

- This simplifies due to the **Geometric Series Formula (0)** $\sum_{t=0}^{m} a \cdot R^t = a(\frac{1-R^{m+1}}{1-R})$, in this case we substitute $\frac{1}{1+r}$ for R, c for a, and n−1 for m.

- This gives us $PV = c\left(\frac{1-(\frac{1}{1+r})^n}{1-\frac{1}{1+r}}\right) = \frac{c(1+r)}{r}\left(1 - (\frac{1}{1+r})^n\right)$

Annuity Present Value (B): $PV = \frac{c(1+r)}{r}\left(1 - (\frac{1}{1+r})^n\right)$

Formula Key:
PV is the **present value** of the annuity
r is the **interest rate**
c is the **payment amount**
n is the **number of payments** in the annuity

Example: You take out a loan with interest rate 6%, and you can afford to make payments of $500 per year for 8 years, with payments at the beginning of the year.

- Here c = 500, r = 0.06, n = 8, which we can plug into **Annuity Present Value (B)**
- Therefore, $PV = \frac{c(1+r)}{r}\left(1 - (\frac{1}{1+r})^n\right) = \frac{500(1.06)}{0.06}\left(1 - (\frac{1}{1.06})^8\right) = 3291.19$

17. How much can you borrow from your aunt today if she will charge you interest at a rate of 33% and you pay will her $150 per year for 11 years at the beginning of each year?

$$\frac{150(1.33)}{.33}\left(1 - \left(\frac{1}{1.33}\right)^{11}\right) = \$578.30$$

For present value too, the calculation is different if payments are made at the end of the year.

- For a series of payments of c dollars for n years at rate r, made at the end of the year:
- $PV = \sum_{t=1}^{n} \frac{c}{(1+r)^t}$

148

- This simplifies due to **Geometric Series formula (1)**: $\sum_{t=1}^{n} a \cdot R^t = a\left(\frac{1-R^n}{\frac{1}{R}-1}\right)$, where we substitute $\frac{1}{1+r}$ for R, and c for a

- Therefore, $PV = c\left(\frac{1-\left(\frac{1}{1+r}\right)^n}{\frac{1}{1+r}-1}\right) = \frac{c}{r}\left(1 - \frac{1}{(1+r)^n}\right)$

Annuity Present Value (E): $PV = \frac{c}{r}\left(1 - \frac{1}{(1+r)^n}\right)$

Formula Key:

PV is the **present value** of the annuity

r is the **interest rate**

c is the **payment amount**

n is the **number of payments** in the annuity

Example: Return to the case where you take out a loan with interest rate 6%, with payments of $500 per year for 8 years, but this time with payments at the *end* of the year.

- You must apply one year of discounting to the first payment, two years' discounting to the second payment etc.

- For the nth payment: $PV = \frac{500}{(1.06)^n}$

- Summing them gives us the total value of the initial loan: $PV = \sum_{i=1}^{8} \frac{500}{(1.06)^i}$

18. How much can you borrow from your Aunt today if she will charge you interest at a rate of 33% and you pay will her $150 per year for 11 years – this time with payments at the end of the year?

$$\frac{150}{.33}\left(1 - \frac{1}{(1.33)^{11}}\right) = \$434.81$$

Warning: Note that the indices are switched around for present value and future value calculations:

- For present value, you start the summation at 0 if payments are made at the **beginning** of the year, and at 1 if payments are made at the **end** of the year.

- For future value, you start the summation at 0 if payments are made at the **end** of the year and at 1 if payments are made at the **beginning** of the year.

The same formula applies when calculating the present value of a series of payments you receive.

Example: Suppose you win a lottery prize that pays you $10,000 a year for 20 years, with payments made at the end of the year. What is the present value of the prize, with a discounting rate of 5%?

- We know that $c = 10000$, $r = 0.05$ and $n = 20$, so $PV = \frac{10000}{0.05}\left(1 - \frac{1}{(1.05)^{20}}\right) = 124{,}622$

19. You uncover corruption in the selection process for the *Park Slope Organic Vegetable Awards*. The organizers offer to bribe you and pay you $1200 at the end of each year for 20 years if you keep quiet. What is the present value of the hush money with a discounting rate of 4.2%?

Unit 3 Topic 3 Check for Understanding

Section 1

[Word Bank: Compound, Payments, Geometric, Arithmetic, Polar, Annuities, Taxes, Interest]

34. Calculating the present value of a cash flow with simple interest requires summing a _geometric_ series.

35. You need to sum a geometric series in order to calculate the present value of a cash flow with _Compound_ interest.

36. Series of equal payments made at regular intervals are called _annuities_

Section 2

37. You deposit $1200 per year, at the start of the year, in a savings account that earns 3.5% interest with annual compounding. $n=25, \ c=1200, \ r=.035$

   a. Express the future value of this payment series in sigma notation.

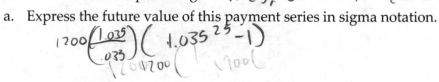

$$1200\left(\frac{1.035}{.035}\right)\left(1.035^{25}-1\right)$$

   b. Calculate the future value of this payment series using the appropriate formula.

   $$= \$48375.72$$

38. You borrow $5000 per year, at the end of the year, at 6.2% interest with annual compounding for seven years.

   a. Express the future value of this payment series in sigma notation.

   $$\left(\frac{5000}{.062}\right)\left(1.062^{7}-1\right)$$

   b. Calculate the future value of this payment series using the appropriate formula.

   $$=\$42225.99$$

39. Your uncle offers you a birthday present of a payment of $50 per year for 20 years, at the end of each year. Your discounting rate is 7%

   a. Express the present value of this payment series in sigma notation.

   $$\frac{50}{.07}\left(1-\left(\frac{1}{1.07}\right)^{20}\right)$$

   b. Calculate the present value of this payment series using the appropriate formula.

   $$=\$1589.10$$

40. You make payments of $350 per year for 12 years, at the start of each year. Your discounting rate is 4.8%

    a. Express the present value of this payment series in sigma notation.

$$350\left(\frac{1.048}{.048}\right)\left(1-\left(\frac{1}{1.048}\right)^{12}\right)$$

$$= \$3288.02$$

    b. Calculate the present value of this payment series using the appropriate formula.

 Spreadsheet Connection

Complete 'Unit 3 Topic 3 Check Sheet'.

TOPIC 4 – MORTGAGES

One particularly important kind of annuity is a **mortgage.**

A **mortgage** is a loan given by a bank for an individual to purchase a house.
- It is paid back in regular installments.
- The house is used as **collateral** on the debt – the bank will take the house if you are unable to make your payments.

There are a number of key terms you need to know when considering a **mortgage**:
- **Principal**: The initial value of the loan.
- **Term**: This how long it takes to completely pay off the loan.
  - The typical mortgage in the US has a 30-year term.
- **Interest**: This may be fixed or adjustable.
  - A **fixed-rate mortgage** has a constant interest rate over the term of the loan.
  - An **adjustable-rate mortgage** has an interest rate that may move up or down over the term of the loan.
- **Down payment**: In order to secure the loan, you must pay a certain amount towards the house up front – this is the down payment.
  - **Loan to value ratio**: This tells you what proportion of the value of the house the loan will cover (you must cover the rest with the down payment).
- **Payments**: This is how much must be paid back towards the debt each period.
- **Debt to income ratio**: This is the proportion of income that is spent on the mortgage and other loan payments.

[Word Bank: house, pony, 50 years, down-payment, principal, mortgage, super-intendent, 30 years, interest]

1. A ___mortgage___ is a loan used to purchase a house.

2. The collateral on the loan is the ___house___

3. The typical term of a mortgage is ___30 years___

4. The amount you initially borrow is the ___principal___

5. The value of the house you buy is equal to the principal + ___down-payment___

6. To determine how much your loan payment must be, you multiply your income by [Circle the correct response]:
   a. The loan to value ratio
   b. The debt to income ratio
   c. The income to loan ratio
   d. The interest to inflation ratio

7. What happens if you are unable to repay the loan?

   You lose the house

8. How do you pay back the mortgage? [Circle the correct response]
   a. All at once
   b. With your soul
   c. Never
   d. In regular installments

Example: You have saved up $70,000 for a down-payment, and you are taking out a mortgage with a loan to value ratio of 80%.
   - This means the mortgage will cover 80% of the value of the house (V), so the down payment must cover the remaining 20%
   - Therefore, $0.2V = 70000$
   - Therefore, $V = 70000/0.2 = 350,000$
   - The value of the loan is 80% of the value of the house, $350,000 * 0.8 = 280,000$

9. You have saved up $45,000 for a down-payment on your dream home, and you are taking out a mortgage with a loan to value ratio of 90%. What is the value of your house and your loan?

   (45000) 45000/.1   450000 · .90
                       = 405000

Example: Your income is $4000 per month, and you take out a mortgage with a debt to income ratio of 35%.
   - This means your monthly mortgage payments will be equal to 35% of your income
   - Therefore, your payments will be $0.35 \cdot 4500 = 1400$

10. Your income is $9200 per month, and you take out a mortgage with a debt to income ratio of 20%. How much will your monthly loan payments be?

    .20 · 9200 = $1840

Calculating Mortgages

To calculate the value of house a person can afford, we work backwards from their income and the terms of the mortgage.

Example: Your income is $4000 per month, and you take out a mortgage with the following terms:

- 35% debt to income ratio
- 80% loan to value ratio
- 30 year term (360 months)
- 5% interest rate (0.42% monthly)

Note: When working with monthly payments, we need to use the monthly interest rate, which is the APR divided by 12.

Stage 1: Calculate the monthly payments: We saw above that the monthly payment in this case is: $0.35 \cdot 4000 = \$1400$

Stage 2: Calculate the value of the loan. You could do this in a spreadsheet, in the same way we saw with annuities:

Payment No.	PV Factor	PV	Rate	0.42%
1	0.995851	1394.191	Payment	1400
2	0.991718	1388.406		
3	0.987603	1382.645		
4	0.983506	1376.908		
5	0.979425	1371.194		
6	0.975361	1365.505		
7	0.971313	1359.839		
8	0.967283	1354.196		
9	0.963269	1348.577		
10	0.959272	1342.981		
*	*	*		
*	*	*		
*	*	*		
355	0.228529	319.9401		
356	0.22758	318.6126		
357	0.226636	317.2905		

358	0.225696	315.974
359	0.224759	314.6629
360	0.223827	313.3572
Total		260794.3

 Spreadsheet Connection

You can see how this is done in 'Unit 3 Topic 3 Worksheet 1 Mortgage PV'.

Alternatively, you can use the Annuity Formula.

- Your loan will be paid off in a series of monthly payments over 30 years
- Therefore, if we discount the payment series by the interest rate, we can calculate the present value of the loan.
- Since payments are made at the end of the month, we use the **Present Value Annuity Formula (E)**: $PV = \frac{c}{r}(1 - \frac{1}{(1+r)^n})$
- Therefore, $PV = \frac{1400}{0.0042}(1 - \frac{1}{(1.0042)^{360}}) = 260,794$

Stage 3: Calculate the value of the house:

- Since the loan to value ratio is 80%, the principle is 80% of the total house value.
- Therefore, the house value is 259610 / 0.8 = 324,513
- The down payment is 324513 · 0.2 = 64,902

11. Your income is $9200 per month, and you take out a mortgage with the following terms:
    - 20% debt to income ratio
    - 90% loan to value ratio
    - 15 year term
    - 9% interest rate

What is the maximum value house you are able to buy?

Evaluating Mortgages

Taking out a mortgage has very significant consequences – whether it is a good idea for a particular person depends upon their goals and situation.

Some potential downsides:

1. A mortgage decreases **liquidity.**
   a. You will need to use a large amount of cash to pay the down payment – this money will no longer be available to cover other expenses.
   b. The monthly mortgage payments may well be more than rent payment, reducing your monthly disposable income.
2. A mortgage decreases **flexibility.**
   a. It is much harder to move as a homeowner than as a renter – you must sell your house and buy another, which will likely incur significant expenses.
   b. You are committed to paying a minimum monthly amount for the term of the mortgage which makes it much harder to switch to a lower paying job or greater vacation while reducing expenses.
3. With a mortgage, you own the home; therefore, you are responsible for repairs to the home.
   a. The cost of repairs could be significant and could be required at an inconvenient time or when you don't have much extra money

Evaluate how the downsides of a mortgage would affect the people described below (if at all):

12. Emilio, a recent college graduate, has taken a job in a lab in Boston, but is looking to change careers wherever the most exciting opportunity is available.

13. Kelly, a mother whose children have left home, is happy in her long-term work at a law firm.

14. Ava, a young banker living in New York, has sufficient savings for a down payment on a house but is interested in investing in her own business.

Some potential benefits:

1. A mortgage allows you to **build wealth.**
   a. While your cash flow may look similar paying off a mortgage to paying off rent, rent is an expense, while mortgage payments increase wealth – you are purchasing a house in installments (which is an asset).
   b. Houses are likely to *appreciate* over time (though this is not guaranteed and varies across locations).
2. A mortgage increases **stability.**
   a. Mortgage payments are fixed, while landlords may increase rent.
   b. As long as you keep up with payments, you can stay in your house if you own it – if you are renting, the landlord may not renew the lease.

Evaluate how the benefits of a mortgage would affect the people described below (if at all):

15. Emilio has a retirement plan through his job; he does not think he needs to make additional investments at this point for building long term wealth.

16. Kelly has more than enough income to cover everyday expenses, but she is concerned about building up sufficient assets for her retirement.

17. Ava is committed to staying in New York, but she is concerned about the volatility of rent, and would like to stop moving every couple of years.

Recall that you can look up house prices on zillow.com. You can also use many comparison sites to compare mortgages.
- Use these tools to see what kind of mortgage and house would be available to the following characters based on the information provided.
- Look up house prices on Zillow and see what each person would be able to afford.

158

18. Emilio wants to buy an apartment as close to the center of Boston as possible. He has $50,000 saved for a down payment and his income is $8000 per month.

19. Kelly wants to buy a house within commuting distance of Denver. She has $85,000 saved for a down payment and her income is $9200 per month.

20. Ava wants to live in New York City. She has $40,000 saved for a down payment, and her income is $4900 per month.

Amortization

An amortization schedule is a table that allows you to keep track of the status of a loan as it is paid off in installments, by giving you an update with each payment. It's useful for highly significant loans like mortgages.

It includes the following information for each loan payment:
- **Payment number** orders the payments from earliest to latest
- **Payment** tells you the value of the payment
- **Principal** tells you the amount used to reduce the principal of the loan
- **Interest** tells you the amount that went towards paying off the period's interest ([adding together principle and interest always gives you the value of the payment)
- **Balance** tells you the amount remaining on the loan after the payment - this allows you to calculate your liabilities at any point over the term of the loan.

Suppose you take out a loan for $10,000 with 4.1% interest. You will pay it back over 10 years with a series of annual payments. Here's an amortization schedule for this loan.
- (The **present value annuity formula** tells us that the annual payments will be $1239.05)

Payment Number	Payment	Principal	Interest	Balance
1	($1,239.05)	($829.05)	($410.00)	$9,170.95
2	($1,239.05)	($863.05)	($376.01)	$8,307.90
3	($1,239.05)	($898.43)	($340.62)	$7,409.47
4	($1,239.05)	($935.27)	($303.79)	$6,474.20
5	($1,239.05)	($973.61)	($265.44)	$5,500.59
6	($1,239.05)	($1,013.53)	($225.52)	$4,487.06
7	($1,239.05)	($1,055.09)	($183.97)	$3,431.97
8	($1,239.05)	($1,098.34)	($140.71)	$2,333.63
9	($1,239.05)	($1,143.38)	($95.68)	$1,190.25
10	($1,239.05)	($1,190.25)	($48.80)	$0.00

Reminder: (100) is another way of writing -100

160

Vocabulary Check:

[Wordbank: payment, principal, interest, balance, remaining, subtracted]

21. The balance refers to the amount _____ on the loan.

22. The principal column lists the amount paid toward the _____ of the loan with a payment.

23. The amount of interest accrued in a period is listed in the _____ column

24. The value of the payment in a given row is equal to the principal + the _____ in that row.

Spreadsheet Connection

Learn to calculate mortgage amortization in the spreadsheet, 'Unit 3 Topic 3 Worksheet 2 Mortgage Amortization'.

Extension: Car Purchase

Example: Ava has just moved to Ohio and needs to buy a car. She is trying to work out what her options are:

- She has $5000 in cash savings, and $500 in surplus income per month.
- She must choose between taking out an **auto-loan**, **leasing** a car, or buying one outright.

Auto-Loan: Often when buying a car, you will need to take out a loan. An **auto-loan** has a similar structure to a mortgage.

- You repay the loan in equal monthly installments over a fixed period of time – usually 3-5 years
- A down payment is required.
- The car is used as collateral on the loan.
- When the loan is fully repaid, you have full ownership of the car.

Example: Ava uses a loan of $20,000 to buy a car for $24,000. The loan has a 36-month term, and an interest rate of 4.8%.

- This means that over 36 equal payments, Ava will repay the $20,000 principal while it is accruing interest at a rate of 4.8%.
- We can model this with an **amortization schedule** just as we did with mortgages.

Spreadsheet Connection

See 'Unit 3 Topic 3 Worksheet 3 Car Payments' for a demonstration of this.
- We see from the amortization schedule that this would result in monthly payments of $597 for Ava.

Ava thinks it might be difficult to afford payments of nearly $600 per month, so she wonders whether there is another option.

 Car Lease: With a **car lease** you loan a car for a fixed period of time, during which you make fixed monthly payments.
- At the end of this period, you must return the car.
- You are also responsible for paying compensation if you damage the car.

Example: Ava is able to find a lease for a comparable car with payments of $350 per month for 36 months.

Deciding on Loan vs Lease:

The key advantage of an **auto-loan** is that you own the car – you can keep it without having to make further payments.
- In other words, you obtain an asset.
- This potentially provides greater value in long run.

On the other hand, a lease will tend to have lower monthly payments, and in addition comes with less risk.
- At the end of one lease, you can get lease on a newer car, so you can continue to use a reliable new vehicle.
- With a loan, you will have to take on the time and risk of selling your car in order to upgrade
- Also, with a loan, you are responsible if the car is faulty since you own it.

 Spreadsheet Connection

From a financial perspective, we can compare present value of costs associated with loan compared with lease.
- See 'Unit 3 Topic 3 Worksheet 3 Car Payments' for a demonstration of this.

162

A final option for Ava is buying a cheap car outright, using her savings.

- This will reduce costs.
- However, an older car is likely to have higher maintenance costs.
- There is also greater risk of needing to unexpectedly get a new car, as well as the stress of driving an unreliable vehicle.
- See 'Unit 3 Topic 3 Worksheet 3 Car Payments' to see the comparison of costs for buying a car outright, against other options.

Extension

You can look up typical car prices on websites like 'Kelley Blue Book'

- https://www.kbb.com/car-values/

Pick out three cars and find their prices, make sure they include:

- A luxury 'dream car'
- A new, or nearly new, car that is less luxurious
- An old cheaper car

25. Fill in the first three columns in the table below:

Car Type	Car Age	Car Price	Monthly Payment

26. Assume you take out an auto loan for the car with a 10% down payment, term of 48 months, and interest rate of 5.1%. Create an amortization table for this in a spreadsheet, then use this to complete the table.

Unit 3 Topic 4 Check for Understanding

Section 1

[Wordbank: principal, collateral, term, home, changes]

1. A mortgage is a loan taken out to buy a _____.
2. Because the bank may take your house if you fail to repay the loan, the house acts as _____ on a mortgage.
3. The _____ of a mortgage tells you how long it will take to pay it off.
4. An adjustable rate mortgage has an interest rate that _____ over the course of the loan.
5. The _____ is the initial value of the loan.

Section 2

6. Which of the following are potential benefits of taking out a mortgage [Circle the correct response(s)]

   a. It increases your liquidity.
   b. It increases the stability of your living situation.
   c. It allows you to build your net worth.
   d. It offers flexibility in where you want to live.

Section 3

7. You want to buy a house worth $267,000 and are offered a mortgage with a loan to value ratio of 80%. What will the down payment on the house be?

8. You are offered a mortgage with a debt to income ratio of 35%; your monthly income is $3800. What is the most you can have as a monthly payment on the loan?

164

9. You take out a 30-year mortgage with monthly payments of $1000 and an interest rate of 5.4% (at the **end** of the month). What is the principal on the mortgage?

10. Your monthly income is $6300 per month. You can take out a mortgage with a 30-year term, debt to income ratio of 35%, and fixed rate interest of 4.9%, with payments at the **beginning** of the month. What is the principal of your loan?

11. You're looking at a mortgage with a debt to income ratio of 30%, fixed rate interest of 5.5%, 30-year term, payments at the **end** of the month, and loan to value ratio of 90%. If your monthly income is $5800, what's the maximum value for a house you are able to buy?

 Spreadsheet Connection

Complete 'Unit 3 Topic 3 Check Sheet'.

TOPIC 5: GROWING CASH FLOW

So far, we have been discussing *constant* cash flows – where the payments are of the same amount each time. Often, though, we have to evaluate *growing* cash flows – where the value of the payment increases over time, by a certain percentage each period.

Example: As a lottery prize you receive $1000 in the first year, and receive 1% more each year for 12 years, at the start of the year.
- In the 7th year you receive $1000 \cdot 1.01^6 = 1061$
- At the nth year, you will receive $1000 \cdot 1.01^{n-1}$

1. Often, a person's payments into a retirement account form a growing cash flow. Why do you think that the payments increase over the course of a person's career?

Example: Return to the lottery prize – you want to evaluate the **present value** of the cash flow, and you have a discounting rate of 3%.
- The present value of the 7th payment is $1061 \cdot 1.03^{-6} = 889$
- To evaluate the present value of the nth payment, we calculate $1000 \cdot \dfrac{1.01^{n-1}}{1.03^{n-1}}$
- We sum these to get the present value of the total cash flow:

$$PV = \sum_{t=1}^{t=12} 1000 \cdot \frac{1.01^{t-1}}{1.03^{t-1}} = \sum_{t=0}^{t=11} 1000 \cdot \frac{1.01^{t}}{1.03^{t}}$$

2. At the start of each year for 5 years, you put aside cash in a shoe box. Your first payment is $250; each year you increase the amount you invest by 5%, and you have a discounting rate of 3.5%. Write a summation (using sigma notation) that expresses the present value of this payment series - you do not have to calculate the amount.

We can present the payment series in a table, as we did with annuities. This time, we need to account for the growth of each payment as well as the discounting.

The **growth factor** is how much bigger, proportionally, a payment is than the original payment.

- Payment value = First payment*growth factor
- The 7th payment of the lottery prize has a growth factor of approximately 1.06
- This gives us the following table for the lottery example

Payment no.	Growth Factor	Payment	PV Factor	PV
1	1.00	$ 1,000.00	1.00	$ 1,000.00
2	1.01	$ 1,010.00	0.97	$ 980.58
3	1.02	$ 1,020.10	0.94	$ 961.54
4	1.03	$ 1,030.30	0.92	$ 942.87
5	1.04	$ 1,040.60	0.89	$ 924.56
6	1.05	$ 1,051.01	0.86	$ 906.61
7	1.06	$ 1,061.52	0.84	$ 889.01
8	1.07	$ 1,072.14	0.81	$ 871.74
9	1.08	$ 1,082.86	0.79	$ 854.82
10	1.09	$ 1,093.69	0.77	$ 838.22
11	1.10	$ 1,104.62	0.74	$ 821.94
12	1.12	$ 1,115.67	0.72	$ 805.98
			Total	$ 10,797.88

3. Fill in the table for the payments of the shoebox scenario from the question above:

Payment No.	Growth Factor	Payment	PV Factor	PV
1				
2				
3				
4				
5				

Payments are often made at the end of the period, which changes the calculations.

Example: Suppose in the lottery case, you receive your payments at the end of the year rather than at the beginning, while all else remains the same.

- Now the first payment must be discounted for one period to calculate its present value:

$$PV = \frac{1000}{1.03}$$

- The second payment must be discounted for **two** periods to calculate present value:
$$PV = 1000 \cdot \frac{1.01}{1.03^2}$$
- In general, the nth payment will only be subject to *n-1* rounds of growth, but will be subject to *n* rounds of discounting, therefore $PV = 1000 \cdot \frac{1.01^{n-1}}{1.03^n}$
- Therefore, the present value of the cash flow is $PV = \sum_{t=1}^{t=12} 1000 \cdot \frac{1.01^{t-1}}{1.03^t}$

Again, we can display this in a table:

Payment no.	Growth Factor	Payment	PV Factor	PV
1	1.00	$ 1,000.00	0.97	$ 970.87
2	1.01	$ 1,010.00	0.94	$ 952.02
3	1.02	$ 1,020.10	0.92	$ 933.54
4	1.03	$ 1,030.30	0.89	$ 915.41
5	1.04	$ 1,040.60	0.86	$ 897.63
6	1.05	$ 1,051.01	0.84	$ 880.20
7	1.06	$ 1,061.52	0.81	$ 863.11
8	1.07	$ 1,072.14	0.79	$ 846.35
9	1.08	$ 1,082.86	0.77	$ 829.92
10	1.09	$ 1,093.69	0.74	$ 813.80
11	1.10	$ 1,104.62	0.72	$ 798.00
12	1.12	$ 1,115.67	0.70	$ 782.51
			Total	$ 10,483.38

4. At the *end* of each year for 5 years, you put aside cash in a shoe box. Your first payment is $250; each year you increase the amount you invest by 5%, and you have a discounting rate of 3.5%. Write a summation (using sigma notation) that expresses the present value of this payment series - you do *not* have to calculate the amount.

5. Fill out the table below for this payment series:

Payment No.	Growth Factor	Payment	PV Factor	PV
1				
2				
3				
4				
5				

Spreadsheet Connection

We can efficiently model PV for growing payment series in spreadsheets. See 'Unit 3 Topic 4 Worksheet 1 - Growing Cash Flows PV'

Alternatively, we can calculate the value of growing payment series by applying the **geometric series formulas**.

Example: Return to the lottery example above with payments made at the ends of the year. We know:

$$PV = \sum_{t=0}^{t=11} 1000 \cdot \frac{1.01^t}{1.03^t}$$

- We can calculate PV using the **Geometric Series Formula (0)**: $a = 1000$, $R = \frac{1.01}{1.03}$, $n = 11$

- $PV = a\left(\frac{1-R^{n+1}}{1-R}\right) = 1000\left(\frac{1-\frac{1.01^{12}}{1.03}}{1-\frac{1.01}{1.03}}\right) = 10{,}800$

Speaking generally, we need to calculate a series of n payments that grow at rate g, with initial payment c, and discounting rate r.

- The calculation depends on whether the payments are made at the beginning or the end of the period.

- If they are at the beginning of the period $PV = \sum_{t=0}^{t=n-1} c \cdot \left(\frac{1+g}{1+r}\right)^t$

- Using the **Geometric Series Formula** $PV = a\left(\frac{1-R^{n+1}}{1-R}\right) = c\left(\frac{1-\left(\frac{1+g}{1+r}\right)^n}{1-\frac{1+g}{1+r}}\right)$

- This simplifies to $PV = \frac{c(1+r)}{r-g}\left(1 - \frac{(1+g)^n}{(1+r)^n}\right)$

6. Calculate the present value of the series of shoe box deposits, described above, using the geometric series formula, with payments made at the beginning of the year from the question above.

Now look at what happens with payments made at the end of the year:

Example: Consider the version of the lottery case in which you receive your payments at the end of the year rather than at the beginning, while all else remains the same.

- We showed above that the present value of the cash flow is $PV = \sum_{t=1}^{t=12} 1000 \cdot \frac{1.01^{t-1}}{1.03^t}$
- We need to rearrange a little to get the geometric series formula:
- $PV = \sum_{t=1}^{t=12} \frac{1000}{1.03} \cdot \frac{1.01^{t-1}}{1.03^{t-1}} = \frac{1000}{1.03} \left(\frac{1-\left(\frac{1.01}{1.03}\right)^{12}}{1-\frac{1.01}{1.03}} \right) = 10,480$

In general, when payments are made at the end of the year, $PV = \sum_{t=1}^{t=n} c \frac{(1+g)^{t-1}}{(1+r)^t}$

- To rearrange: $PV = \sum_{t=1}^{t=n} \frac{c}{1+r} \frac{(1+g)^{t-1}}{(1+r)^{t-1}}$

- Applying the geometric series formula $PV = \frac{c}{1+r} \left(\frac{1-\left(\frac{1+g}{1+r}\right)^n}{1-\frac{1+g}{1+r}} \right)$

- Simplifying $PV = \frac{c}{r-g} [1 - \frac{(1+g)^n}{(1+r)^n}]$

This is known as the **growing payment formula**:

Growing Payment Formula: $PV = \frac{c}{r-g} [1 - \frac{(1+g)^n}{(1+r)^n}]$

Formula Key:

PV is the **present value** of the cash flow

c is the **payment amount**

r is the **discounting rate**

g is the **growth rate**

n is the **number of payments**

Example: Your little brother wants you to sneak him into your high school prom. In return, he offers to give you annual payments (at the end of each year) for fifteen years. The first payment will be $35, and the payments will grow by 15% each year. You have a discounting rate of 3.8%. What is the present value of this payment series?

- We can use the growing payment formula: $c = 35$; $g = 0.15$; $r = 0.038$; $n = 15$

- $PV = \frac{c}{r-g}\left[1 - \frac{(1+g)^n}{(1+r)^n}\right] = \frac{35}{0.038-0.15}\left[1 - \frac{(1.15)^{15}}{(1.038)^{15}}\right] = 1140$

Analysis: Should you agree to your brother's offer? Since the value of his cash flow is $1140, it depends whether the embarrassment of having him with you at the prom is worth more or less than that for you.

7. Suppose you make the shoe box deposits at the end of the year instead, while all else remains the same. Now calculate the present value of the payment series.

8. Your little sister wants a loan from you so she can go to Vegas for Spring Break. She can repay you over 15 years, with payments at the end of each year. The first payment will be $180, the growth rate will be 5.8%. If you have a discounting rate of 8.9%, how much should you loan her?

9. You want to take out a loan to buy a car. You will repay the loan over 8 years, with a first annual payment of $1500 and a growth rate of 2.5%, and payments at the end of the year. The loan has an interest rate of 5.4%. What value loan can you take out?

Growing Payment Future Value

We also need to calculate the future value of a payment series.

Example: You are saving for a down payment on a house with annual investments (at the end of the year). You will make an initial investment of $3,000 and your payments will grow by 3% each year for 10 years – your investments will earn interest at a rate of 5.1%. We need to calculate how much you will have available for a down payment after 10 years.

- The first payment is $3000, and it earns interest for 9 years, so its future value is $3000 \cdot 1.051^9 = 4694$

- The nth payment has a value of $3000 \cdot 1.03^{n-1}$, and it earns interest for $10-n$ years, so its future value is $3000 \cdot 1.03^{n-1} \cdot 1.051^{10-n}$
- Therefore, future value of the payment series is $\sum_{t=1}^{t=10} 3000 \cdot 1.03^{t-1} \cdot 1.051^{10-t}$

We can again put this in a table.
- The **growth factor** is the same as before, since the value at the time of payment does not change, regardless of whether we are calculating present value or future value.
- The **future value** factor is exactly the same as with annuities.

Payment no.	Growth Factor	Payment	FV Factor	FV
1	1.00	$ 3,000.00	1.56	$ 4,694.03
2	1.03	$ 3,090.00	1.49	$ 4,600.24
3	1.06	$ 3,182.70	1.42	$ 4,508.32
4	1.09	$ 3,278.18	1.35	$ 4,418.24
5	1.13	$ 3,376.53	1.28	$ 4,329.96
6	1.16	$ 3,477.82	1.22	$ 4,243.44
7	1.19	$ 3,582.16	1.16	$ 4,158.65
8	1.23	$ 3,689.62	1.10	$ 4,075.56
9	1.27	$ 3,800.31	1.05	$ 3,994.13
10	1.30	$ 3,914.32	1.00	$ 3,914.32
			Total	$ 42,936.88

10. You are offered a series of loans to cover expenses while you're a student. You borrow $5000 the first year (at the end of the year), the loan value increases by 8% each year for 5 years and earns 11% interest. You want to know how much you will owe after 5 years, assuming you do not make any payments in this time. Write the future value of your debt as a summation.

$$FV_5 = 5000 \left(PV_{5.08} R_5\right) \left[1 - \frac{(1+g)^{\wedge}}{(1+r)^{\wedge}}\right]$$

$$= \frac{5000}{.11-.08} \left[\frac{1-(1.08)^5}{(1.11)}\right]$$

$$= \$21,337.55$$

11. Fill in the table below for this cash flow:

Payment No.	Growth Factor	Payment	FV Factor	FV
1				
2				
3				
4				
5				

To get a complete picture of the value of a payment series, we can create a single table that combines information of both PV and FV of a payment series.

- When doing this the discounting rate must be the same for PV factor as for FV factor.

Example: Recall the series of savings for the down payment. Here's the full table:

Payment no.	Growth Factor	Payment	PV Factor	PV	FV Factor	FV
1	1.00	$ 3,000.00	0.95	$ 2,854.42	1.56	$ 4,694.03
2	1.03	$ 3,090.00	0.91	$ 2,797.39	1.49	$ 4,600.24
3	1.06	$ 3,182.70	0.86	$ 2,741.50	1.42	$ 4,508.32
4	1.09	$ 3,278.18	0.82	$ 2,686.72	1.35	$ 4,418.24
5	1.13	$ 3,376.53	0.78	$ 2,633.03	1.28	$ 4,329.96
6	1.16	$ 3,477.82	0.74	$ 2,580.42	1.22	$ 4,243.44
7	1.19	$ 3,582.16	0.71	$ 2,528.86	1.16	$ 4,158.65
8	1.23	$ 3,689.62	0.67	$ 2,478.34	1.10	$ 4,075.56
9	1.27	$ 3,800.31	0.64	$ 2,428.82	1.05	$ 3,994.13
10	1.30	$ 3,914.32	0.61	$ 2,380.29	1.00	$ 3,914.32
			Total	$ 26,109.79	Total	$ 42,936.88

12. Complete the full table for the cash flow in which you borrow $5000 the first year (at the end of the year), the loan value increases by 8% each year for 5 years, and accrues 11% interest.

Payment No.	Growth Factor	Payment	PV Factor	PV	FV Factor	FV
1						
2						
3						
4						
5						

Spreadsheet Connection

We can efficiently model FV for growing payment series in spreadsheets. See 'Unit 3 Topic 4 Worksheet 1 - Growing Cash Flows FV'

Again, we can also calculate future value by applying the geometric series formula.

Example: Recall the investment for a down payment from the example above. The future value of the payment series is given by the following sum:

$$\sum_{t=1}^{t=10} 3000 \cdot 1.03^t \cdot 1.051^{10-t}$$

We need to find a way to apply the **geometric series formula**.

- To do this, we need the formula being summed to consist of a constant a, and a single term R being raised to the power of t.
- To get this, we rearrange by taking out a factor of 1.051^9
- This gives us $FV = 1.051^9 \sum_{t=1}^{t=10} 3000 \cdot 1.03^{t-1} \cdot 1.051^{-t-1} = 1.051^{10} \sum_{t=1}^{t=10} 3000 \cdot (\frac{1.03}{1.051})^{t-1}$
- Now applying the **geometric series formula**, we get $FV = \frac{3000 \cdot 1.051^{10}}{0.051 - 0.03} (1 - (\frac{1.03}{1.051})^{10}) = 42,900$

In general, for a payment series with initial payment c, growth rate g, interest rate r, and number of payments n, the future value is given by the following summation:

$$\sum_{t=1}^{t=n} c \cdot (1+g)^{t-1} \cdot (1+r)^{n-t}$$

- As before, we need to rearrange, before we can apply the **geometric series formula.**
- This gives us $FV = (1+r)^{n-1} \sum_{t=1}^{t=n} c \cdot (\frac{1+g}{1+r})^{t-1}$

174

- Applying the geometric series formula gives us: $FV = \frac{c(1+r)^n}{r-g}\left(1 - \left(\frac{1+g}{1+r}\right)^n\right)$

Growing Payment Future Value: $FV = \frac{c(1+r)^n}{r-g}\left(1 - \left(\frac{1+g}{1+r}\right)^n\right)$

Formula Key:

PV is the **present value** of the cash flow

r is the **discounting rate**

g is the **growth rate**

c is the **payment amount**

n is the **number of payments**

Note: the **Growing Payment Future Value** formula is just the **growing payment formula** for present value multiplied by $(1 + r)^n$

Extra Credit:

13. Why is the **Growing Payment Future Value** formula simply the **growing payment formula** for present value multiplied by $(1 + r)^n$?

14. You take out a loan at the end of each year. You borrow $5000 the first year and the loan value increases by 8% each year for 5 years, while accruing 11% interest. Calculate the future debt from this series of loans.

Note: This is the same problem used in the example above. Use the work you've done.

15. Jerry plans to make annual contributions to a fund for when his children go to college. He invests $1800 the first year. His investments grow by 4% each year, and earn interest at a rate of 2.5%. How much will be available for his children after 18 years?

Limits

We can also ask about the value of a sequence of payments made *in perpetuity* – that is they never stop. For example, you might receive lottery payments of $1500 every year indefinitely.

A sequence of constant payments that doesn't stop is called a **perpetuity.**

Example: Both the US government and the Bank of England, issued **perpetuities** in the 18th century.

To calculate the present value of such payments, you must take the *limit* of the **Present Value Annuity Formula (E):** $PV = \frac{c}{r}\left(1 - \frac{1}{(1+r)^n}\right)$

- That is: $PV = \lim_{n \to \infty} \frac{c}{r}\left(1 - \frac{1}{(1+r)^n}\right)$
- Since $\lim_{n \to \infty} \frac{1}{(1+r)^n} = 0$, $PV = \frac{c}{r}$

Perpetuity Formula: $\boldsymbol{PV = \frac{c}{r}}$

Formula Key:

PV is the **present value** of the perpetuity
r is the **discounting rate**
c is the **payment amount**

Example: You receive annual lottery payments of $1500 in perpetuity; your discounting rate is 8.2%. What is the present value of the perpetuity?

- Applying the perpetuity formula $PV = \frac{c}{r} = \frac{1500}{0.082} = 18{,}292.68$

16. The British government agrees to pay you $12000 per year in perpetuity (it can be passed down to your heirs). You have a discounting rate of 4.5%. What is the present value of the perpetuity?

$$\frac{12000}{.045} = \$26{,}666.67$$

17. Your uncle is willing to buy the perpetuity from you for $47,000. What is your uncle's discounting rate?

$47000 = \frac{12000}{R}$ $=.9\%$ $\frac{47000R = 12000}{47000} = 25.5\%$

We can again investigate the limit if growing payments are made in perpetuity. This time, take the limit of the **growing payment formula:** $PV = \frac{c}{r-g}\left(1 - \frac{(1+g)^n}{(1+r)^n}\right)$

- $PV = \lim_{n \to \infty} \frac{c}{r-g} \left(1 - \frac{(1+g)^n}{(1+r)^n}\right) = \frac{c}{r-g}$
- This is known as the **Dividend Discount Formula.**

Dividend Discount Formula: $PV = \dfrac{c}{r-g}$

Formula Key:

PV is the **present value** of the perpetuity

r is the **discounting rate**

c is the **payment amount**

g is the **growth rate**

Example: You are offered a series of payments that start at $400, grow by 3% each year, and never end. Your discounting rate is 6%. We can apply the dividend discount formula to calculate the present value:

- $c = 400$, $r = 0.06$, $g = 0.03$
- $PV = \dfrac{c}{r-g} = \dfrac{400}{.06 - .03} = 13,333.33$

18. You and your heirs must pay your sister and her heirs a series of payments that begin at $50 and grow by 4.5% each year. Your discounting rate is 7.2%. What is the present value of this payment series? $PV = ?$

$$\frac{50}{.072 - .045} \qquad \frac{50}{.027} = 1851.85$$

19. In exchange for eternal life, you must make annual payments to the devil. The first payment is $2300 and they grow by 4%. Your discounting rate is 5.1%. What is the present value of this payment series?

$$\frac{2300}{.051 - .04} = \$ \ 209090.91$$

20. The devil makes you a second offer: in exchange for your soul, you will receive a series of payments in perpetuity. The first payment is $17,000, the payments grow at a rate of 1.3% per year and your discounting rate is 5.1%. What is the present value of this payment series?

$$\frac{17000}{.051 - .013} = \$ \ 447368.42$$

 Extension

21. You want eternal life as long as you never go broke; you don't care about selling your soul as long as you never have to face the afterlife; you have access to a savings account with an interest rate of 5.1%. Should you take the devil up on either or both of their offers? Why?

*Why is it called the **Dividend Discount Formula**?* An important kind of growing cash flow comes from **stocks** – when you buy stocks in a company, you will often receive regular, growing payments. These are known as **dividends**. The **Dividend Discount Formula** allows you to calculate the present value of a series of dividend payments.

- Note that the Dividend Discount Formula is only one method among many for valuing stocks – we'll discuss other methods in Unit 5.

Example: You are considering buying shares in *Deals Enterprises*. This will pay annual dividends starting at $120 and growing by 3% per year. If you have a discount rate of 3.4%, what's the most you should pay for these shares?

- This requires we use the **Dividend Discount Formula**: $PV = \frac{120}{0.034-0.03} = 30{,}000$

 22. You own shares in *Big-Time Business* which pays annual dividends starting at $750 and growing by 1% per year. If you have a discount rate of 5.7%, what's the least you should sell these shares for?

 Extension

How did we calculate these formulas?

Start with the **perpetuity** formula. We want to calculate $\lim_{n\to\infty} \frac{c}{r}\left(1 - \frac{1}{(1+r)^n}\right)$

- Since it's n that 'goes to infinity' while the other variables are constant, we should focus on the part of the expression that involves n.
- What happens to the value of $\frac{1}{(1+r)^n}$ as n goes to infinity?
- Because $(1+r) > 1$, the bigger n gets, the smaller $\frac{1}{(1+r)^n}$ gets; in fact, it gets closer and closer to 0.

Now we look at how this affects the whole expression:

- As $\frac{1}{(1+r)^n}$ approaches 0, $(1 - \frac{1}{(1+r)^n})$ approaches 1
- Therefore, as $\frac{1}{(1+r)^n}$ approaches 0, $\frac{c}{r}\left(1 - \frac{1}{(1+r)^n}\right)$ approaches $\frac{c}{r}$
- Putting this all together, we get that $\lim\limits_{n\to\infty} \frac{c}{r}\left(1 - \frac{1}{(1+r)^n}\right) = \frac{c}{r}$

Similarly, for the **dividend discount formula**, we're looking at $\lim\limits_{n\to\infty} \frac{c}{r-g}\left(1 - \frac{(1+g)^n}{(1+r)^n}\right)$

- We start by looking at what happens to $\frac{(1+g)^n}{(1+r)^n}$ when n goes to infinity.

- If r is bigger than g, this also goes to 0, and so similar reasoning to before gives us the **dividend discount formula**.

23. You are offered shares in *Too Good to Be True Inc.* These pay dividends starting at $100 and growing at a rate of 11.1% per year. Your discounting rate is 7.4%. What is the value of this payment series according to the **Dividend Discount Formula**? Is this result correct? Explain your answer.

Unit 3 Topic 5 Check for Understanding

Section 1

[Word Bank: Bonus, Increases, Dividend, Quotient, Perpetuity, Eternally, Decreases]

1. With a growing cash flow, the amount you pay or receive each year _____ over time.
2. A _____ is a cash flow that does not stop.
3. The annual payout from a stock is a _____.

Section 2.

4. Your Uncle promises to give you a series of payments to congratulate you on graduating school. He will give you annual payments for 12 years, at the end of each year; his initial payment will be $150, and payments will grow at a rate of 3%. If your discounting rate is 5.5%, what is the present value of this cash flow?

5. Jerry is saving for a down payment on a mortgage. He plans to save for seven years. His first year he will save $8000, the amount he saves will increase by 3% each year, and his savings will earn 4.3% interest. How much will Jerry have available for a down payment?

6. A mysterious man offers to pay you $1000 per year for the rest of time, in exchange for your dignity (this cash flow will be passed on to you heir) – you have a discounting rate of 4.7%.

    a. How much is this cash flow currently worth?

b. Suppose that this man knows that the world will end (and, he claims, time itself) in the year 2099. So he will only make payments up until then. How much less than you expected are you getting, in terms of present value?

7. You buy stock in *General Cars USA*, your stock offers an initial dividend payment of $80, and the payment will grow at a rate of 3% per year. Your discounting rate is 6.6%.
   a. What is the value of your stock, according to the dividend discount formula?

   b. Your friend proposes a deal where she pays you a sum of money now, and in return she gains ownership of the stock in 15 years' time. What is a fair payment if you make this deal?

TOPIC 6: RETIREMENT

One place we need to put all this together is when calculating how much to save for retirement.

Most people do not work for their entire lives – they stop working when they reach a certain age.

- This period is known as **retirement.**

Example: Maria is 65 years' old – she wants to retire in the next couple of years so she can move nearer her children and spend more time painting.

1. What other reasons might lead someone to retire?

When you retire, you need money available to fund your expenses, though you are no longer earning a wage. This is something you must plan for.

First think about your goals:

- How much, as a percentage of your working income, do you want to be able to spend upon retirement?
- How much do you want your retirement income to grow?
- How long do you estimate you'll be retired for?

Example: Maria wants 60% of her current annual income available when she retires; she wants it to grow by at least 1.5% per year, and she expects to be retired for 25 years.

2. What age would you like to work until? What kinds of things would you like to do when you retire?

In order to meet your goals, you will need to save money while you are working to use when you retire. Think about the financial constraints:

- What is your current salary?
- How much longer will you work?
- How much do you expect your income to grow?
- What rate of return do you expect on your investments?

Example: 20 years ago, Maria calculated that to meet her goals, she needed to start saving $8000 per year for retirement.

- How did Maria come to this figure? She worked backwards from her goals using the appropriate cash-flow formulas.

Making this calculation has two steps:

- **Step 1**: Calculate how much you need saved at the point you retire in order to meet your retirement goals.
- **Step 2**: Calculate how much you need to invest when working to have this amount saved when you retire.

Step 1 Example: Eduardo wants 50% of his annual income available when he retires; he wants it to grow by 1.5% per year, and he expects to be retired for 20 years. How much does he need saved when he retires?

- We need to calculate the present value, at the point of retirement, of the cash flow Eduardo will use to fund his retirement expenses.
- We can do this in a spreadsheet by calculating the present value of his annual retirement expenses, then sum them.

In order to work this out we need to know Eduardo's salary when he retires, and how much interest his retirement savings will earn after he's retired. (We can calculate this from his current salary, and how much he expects it to grow.)

Here's an example of the information you need:

Current Salary	$ 40,000.00
Salary Growth	1.5%
Years till retirement	40
Final Salary	$ 72,560.74
Retirement Factor	50%
Initial Retirement Expense	$ 36,280.37
Retirement Growth	2%
Retirement Years	20
Savings Interest Rate	4%

We can use this to calculate the present value of Eduardo's total retirement expenses, the same way we calculate the present value of any growing cash flow.

The numbers in the column are growing by 2%, the "Retirement Growth"

The numbers in the column are decreasing by 4%, his discount rate.

In a spreadsheet, we get the following table:

Retirement Year	Annual Expense	PV Factor	Expense PV
1	$ 36,280.37	1.00	$ 36,280.37
2	$ 37,005.98	0.96	$ 35,582.67
3	$ 37,746.10	0.92	$ 34,898.39
4	$ 38,501.02	0.89	$ 34,227.26
5	$ 39,271.04	0.85	$ 33,569.05
6	$ 40,056.46	0.82	$ 32,923.49
7	$ 40,857.59	0.79	$ 32,290.34
8	$ 41,674.74	0.76	$ 31,669.38
9	$ 42,508.23	0.73	$ 31,060.35
10	$ 43,358.40	0.70	$ 30,463.04
11	$ 44,225.57	0.68	$ 29,877.21
12	$ 45,110.08	0.65	$ 29,302.65
13	$ 46,012.28	0.62	$ 28,739.13
14	$ 46,932.52	0.60	$ 28,186.46
15	$ 47,871.18	0.58	$ 27,644.41
16	$ 48,828.60	0.56	$ 27,112.79
17	$ 49,805.17	0.53	$ 26,591.39
18	$ 50,801.27	0.51	$ 26,080.02
19	$ 51,817.30	0.49	$ 25,578.48
20	$ 52,853.65	0.47	$ 25,086.58
		Total	$ 607,163.44

3. Eduardo needs to save $602,000 for when he retires – i.e. over half a million dollars. Is that more or less than you would expect to have to save for retirement? Explain why.

Spreadsheet Connection

You can apply what you learned modeling growing cash flows in spreadsheets, to model retirement savings. Complete 'Unit 3 Topic 5 Retirement'.

Since this is a growing cash flow, we can verify our answer using the **growing payment formula**:

$$PV = \frac{c}{r-g}\left[1 - \frac{(1+g)^n}{(1+r)^n}\right]$$

- c is the initial payment, $36,280.30
- $g = 0.02$; $n = 20$
- r is the discounting rate – this is the interest that Eduardo's retirement savings earn before he uses them. In our example, we assume $r = 4\%$.
- Therefore, $PV = \frac{c}{r-g}\left[1 - \frac{(1+g)^n}{(1+r)^n}\right] = \frac{36,280.30}{0.04-0.02}\left[1 - \frac{(1.02)^{20}}{(1.04)^{20}}\right] = 607,163.44$

4. Kelly wants to start with $41,000 annually to cover expenses when she retires, with the annual amount growing by 1.8%; her retirement savings will be in an account that earns 3.7% interest, and she expects to be retired for 22 years. How much should she have saved when she retires?

First answer in a spreadsheet, then verify using the **growing payment formula**.

Step 2 Example: Eduardo needs to have saved $607,163.44 by the time he retires. He will be investing his retirement savings in an account that earns interest at 8.9%. How much does he need to save each year to meet this goal?

- We can use a spreadsheet to calculate the future value of his retirement savings.
- Once the spreadsheet is set up, we can look at whether various savings strategies are sufficient to meet his needs.

Current Salary	$ 40,000.00				Total	$ 769,274.20
Salary Growth	1.5%					
Years until retirement	40		**Work Year**	**Payment**	**FV Factor**	**FV**
Final Salary	$ 72,560.74		1	$ 2,000.00	27.80	$ 55,605.44
Retirement Factor	50%		2	$ 2,030.00	25.53	$ 51,826.93
Initial Retirement Expense	$ 36,280.37		3	$ 2,060.45	23.44	$ 48,305.17
Retirement Growth	2%		4	$ 2,091.36	21.53	$ 45,022.73
Retirement Years	20		5	$ 2,122.73	19.77	$ 41,963.33

Retirement Return	4%		6	$ 2,154.57	18.15	$ 39,111.83
Savings Rate	5%		7	$ 2,186.89	16.67	$ 36,454.09
Investment Return	8.90%		8	$ 2,219.69	15.31	$ 33,976.95
First Payment	$ 2,000.00		9	$ 2,252.99	14.06	$ 31,668.14
			10	$ 2,286.78	12.91	$ 29,516.22
Surplus	$ 162,110.76		11	$ 2,321.08	11.85	$ 27,510.53

The key variable here is savings rate: what percentage of his income Eduardo puts towards retirement.

- The table above shows us that with a rate of 5%, the future value of his retirement savings is $769,274.20
- The surplus box shows the difference between the amount saved and the amount needed for retirement.
    - In this case, Eduardo has saved $162,110.76 more than he needs.
    - If this number is negative, then the savings are not sufficient.

Spreadsheet Connection

Create a spreadsheet model for Eduardo's retirement savings. Look at some different value for savings rate, and whether they allow Eduardo to meet his target. (*Note that for this activity you must start from a black spreadsheet document, rather than using a FiCycle template. If you get stuck, you can look back at the 'Unit 3 Topic 5 Retirement' spreadsheet for a hint.*)

1. After playing with the numbers a little bit in a spreadsheet, what's the lowest savings rate you found that still helps him meet his retirement goal? _____
2. What's his surplus if he saves 6.5%? _____
3. Look at what happens if he decides he wants a different percentage of his final salary for retirement income. Pick a different percentage of his final salary for retirement income and report what percent he needs to save if he wants to meet this new goal (it's okay if there is a surplus).

    Percentage of his final salary for retirement income: _____

    Percent of income that must be saved to meet new target: _____

    Surplus: _____

We can also calculate the value of the initial payment that allows Eduardo to meet his retirement goal **precisely**. This is known as the **break-even** value.

- In this situation we know FV = \$607,163.44; r = 0.89; g = 0.02; n = 40; and we need to calculate c (the initial paymnent).

- We use the **growing payment future value** formula: $FV = \frac{c(1+r)^n}{r-g}(1 - (\frac{1+g}{1+r})^n)$

- Rearranging, $c = \frac{FV}{[1-\frac{(1+g)^n}{(1+r)^n}](1+r)^n} \cdot (r - g) = \frac{607{,}163.44}{[1-\frac{(1.02)^{40}}{(1.089)^{40}}](1.089)^{40}} \cdot (0.089 - 0.02) = 1492.54$

- Therefore, Eduardo must start saving \$1492.54 per year for retirement.

5. Karina is currently earning \$85,000 and she plans to work for another 20 years; her wage will grow 1% each year.
    - Due to a divorce, she does not have any retirement savings built up, so she must rely on saving from her current and future income to meet her retirement goals.
    - Her investments for retirement will earn 10.5% interest.
    - How much must she start saving to meet the retirement goals from the question above?
    - She wants to have \$800,000 in savings at the time she retires.

    a. Create a spreadsheet, giving the future value of her investments, and find a savings rate which gives her a reasonable surplus, and a rate that is insufficient.

    b. Use the growing payment formula to calculate Karina's break-even rate.

6. Marco is deciding on a retirement plan as he starts his first job. He is trying to decide whether to start saving now or wait until he is older.
    - He is tempted to wait until later since he thinks he will have more money to spare then: "I can have more fun when I'm young, so it's best to make the most of the money I have now" he reasons.
    - His starting salary is \$32,000 and he expects it to grow by 3.1% per year for 40 years.
    - He will invest it in a retirement account that earns interest at 9.4%.
    - His goal is to start retirement with 50% of his final salary, and for his annual withdrawals to grow 2%. After he retires, his savings will earn 3.2% interest.

a. Calculate how much Marco needs as an initial investment to meet his retirement goals if he starts saving now. First create a spreadsheet to model his retirement savings and expenses, then verify with the **growing payment formulas**.

7. Calculate how much Marco needs to as an initial investment to meet his retirement goals if he starts saving in 20 years' time. Again, first create a spreadsheet to model his modified retirement savings, then verify with the **growing payment formulas**.

8. What advice would you offer Marco about when he should start saving.

Further Notes on Retirement

Planning for retirement in real life is never quite such a simple decision as the one Marco was making.

Not all the money you will have available upon retiring needs to come from your current wages:

1. Many employers offer retirement benefits where they make a contribution to your retirement savings account (either a fixed amount, or in proportion to what you contribute).

2. There are tax deductions for saving for retirement – income that you invest in a retirement account (an IRA) is not usually taxed – which in effect means the increase in your retirement savings will be greater than the decrease in available wages for you.

3. You get assistance from the government when you retire in the form of Social Security: when you reach retirement age you will start receiving checks from Social Security in return for the Social Security tax payments you made when you were working.

When you are starting your first job, there is a lot of **uncertainty** ahead – your plan for retirement cannot be precisely mapped out for the next 40 years:

- You don't know in advance at what rate your income will grow.
- You don't know what the return on your investments will be.

Calculations using the growing payment formulas, like the ones you did for Marco, should be seen as rough estimates to guide your decision making, not strict plans for your entire financial future.

You need to be flexible in dealing with uncertainty and risk – Unit 4 will discuss how to do this.

9. Your employer matches your retirement contributions, so that for every dollar you save for retirement, they contribute a dollar to your retirement account. How does this affect your plans to meet your retirement goals? Explain your answer.

10. You earn $50,000 a year and your income is taxed at a rate of 25%. You consider contributing $5000 a year to a retirement account, which is not taxed. Compare how this affects your after-tax income and your retirement balance.

11. What are some advantages and disadvantages of having a government issued monthly social security check when you retire, instead of leaving all your retirement saving up to you?

Unit 3 Topic 6 Check for Understanding

Section 1

[Word Bank: deductions, hikes, nominal, real, positive, bribes, negative, match, steal, Social Security, decreases, increases]

1. Employers will often _____ your retirement contributions
2. Retirement contributions are subject to tax _____
3. You may receive financial support from the government in retirement through

_____

Section 2

4. Which of the following factors would *increase* the amount you need to save for retirement? Circle all correct options.
   a. The expected retirement age is raised
   b. Advances in medical science mean that your life expectancy increases
   c. You find an investment option with a higher interest rate
   d. You decide you want to retire earlier

5. What could you do if your current saving plan will not meet your current retirement goals? Circle all correct options.
   a. Increase the amount you save each month
   b. Exercise more
   c. Decrease the fraction of your final salary you aim for as retirement income
   d. Increase the growth rate of your annual investments

Section 3

Janice is currently earning $42,000 and she plans to work for another 30 years; her wage will grow 1.5% each year.

- Her investments for retirement will earn 8.3% interest.
- Her goal is to start retirement with 55% of her final salary, and for her annual withdrawals to grow 1.8%. After she retires, her savings will earn 2.9% interest.
- She plans to be retired for 25 years.

6. Use the growing payment formula to calculate how much she needs to have saved at the point of retirement.

7. Use the growing payment future value formula to calculate how much she must start saving to meet her break-even rate.

 Spreadsheet Connection

Complete 'Unit 3 Topic 5 Check Sheet'

192

Topic 7: Inflation

The value of a dollar does not stay constant when there is inflation. The value of a dollar is observed in terms of purchasing power, which is the real, tangible goods that money can buy. When inflation goes up, there is a decline in the purchasing power of money. For example, if the inflation rate is 2% annually, then theoretically a $1 pack of gum will cost $1.02 in a year. After inflation, your dollar can't buy the same amount of goods as it could beforehand.

Inflation is generally measured in terms of a <u>consumer price index</u> (CPI), which tracks the prices of a basket of core goods and services over time. Viewed another way, this tool measures the "<u>real</u>" — that is, adjusted for inflation — value of earnings over time. It is important to note that the components of the CPI do not change in price at the same rates or even necessarily move in the same direction. For example, the prices of secondary education and housing have been increasing much more rapidly than the prices of other goods and services; meanwhile fuel prices have risen, fallen, risen again and fallen again — each time very sharply — in the past ten years. [From investopedia.com]

 Inflation: The factor by which the dollar-cost of general goods changes over time. **Inflation** affects how we think about the time value of money.

Nominal cash flow: This is the dollar amount coming in and out, not adjusted for inflation.
- **Nominal interest rate** is the percentage change in dollar value over time, without adjusting for inflation.

Real cash flow: This is the cash coming in and out adjusted for inflation.
- $1000 real cash flow is a payment with the purchasing power of $1000 today.
- If inflation is 1.5%, a real cash flow of $1000 in one years' time is a nominal cash flow of $1000 \cdot 1.015 = 1015$
- **Real interest rate** is the percentage change in purchasing power over time, adjusting for inflation.

[Word Bank: Increases, Decreases, More, Less, Positive, Negative, Goods, Bads, Real Cash Flow, Imaginary, Nominal Cash Flow, Significant]

1. When inflation is positive, the purchasing power of money _____ over time.
2. When inflation is negative, you can buy _____ with $1 at a later date.
3. Inflation is measured by checking how the price of _____ changes over time.
4. If shopping for groceries costs you $60, when last year it cost you $54, does this suggest inflation is positive or negative? _____.
5. The inflation adjusted value for a cash flow is known as _____.
6. The cash flow coming in as a non-inflation adjusted dollar value is known as _____.

7. If inflation is 2% and you receive a nominal payment of $30 in one year's time, what is the real cash flow?

8. If, in a year's time, you receive a nominal payment of $150, but the real cash flow is $133, what is the rate of inflation?

9. If inflation is -1.7% and you receive a real payment of $800 in one year's time, what is the nominal payment?

When there is inflation over multiple years, the effect compounds, just like with interest.

Example: You receive a nominal payment of $1000 in two years' time, and annual inflation is 2%.

- The real value of a payment, one year ahead is $1000 \cdot \dfrac{1}{1.02}$
- Therefore, the real value two years ahead is $1000 \cdot \dfrac{1}{1.02}^2$

In general, if there is inflation at rate i, the real value of nominal payment c, made in n years' time is:

$$c \cdot \frac{1}{1+i}^n$$

10. You receive a nominal payment of $30 in 10 years' time. What is the real value of this payment if inflation is 7%?

194

Inflation and Retirement

When inflation rates are high, any cash you have that is not earning interest will lose value at a significant rate.

- This is especially important over multiple years since inflation compounds just like interest.

11. Use the rule of 72 to estimate how long it will take for the real value of money to half if inflation is at 5%.

This consideration is particularly important with respect to retirement savings.

- If you allotted the same dollar amount for retirement expenses, for each year of your retirement, the real value of your retirement savings would decline.
- If you want to maintain the same standard of living over the course of your retirement, your retirement savings will have to grow at least at the rate of inflation (this is why we assumed the retirement expenses grew in the previous section).

12. Maria is planning to use $45,000 per year in retirement expenses (she has forgotten to account for inflation, so she doesn't expect her retirement expenses to grow). If inflation will be 1.8% per year, what is the real value of $45,000 in the 20th year of her retirement?

Historical Inflation Rates

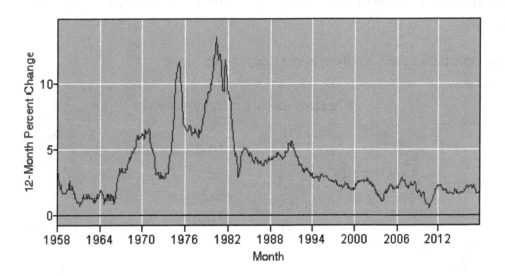

Image: https://data.bls.gov/pdq/SurveyOutputServlet

This graph shows inflation rate in the US over the past 60 years.
- You can see that inflation has been very low recently.
- In the '70s and early '80s inflation was at times over 10%

13. How do you think it would affect your financial planning if inflation was at 10%, so that each year products get 10% more expensive?

Inflation can be a serious problem if it gets too high. It leads to what's known as **hyperinflation**; when this happens, people start to panic and the whole economy might collapse.

The table below shows how extreme this can get.

Highest monthly inflation rates in history						
Country	Currency name	Month with highest inflation rate	Highest monthly inflation rate	Equivalent daily inflation rate	Time required for prices to double	Highest denomination of currency available
Hungary	Hungarian pengő	July 1946	4.19×10^{16} %	207.19%	15.6 hours	100 Quintillion (10^{20})
Zimbabwe	Zimbabwe dollar	November 2008	7.96×10^{10} %	98.01%	24.7 hours	100 Trillion (10^{14})
Yugoslavia	Yugoslav dinar	January 1994	3.13×10^{8} %	64.63%	1.4 days	500 Billion (5×10^{11})
Germany (Weimar Republic)	German Papiermark	October 1923	29,500%	20.87%	3.7 days	100 Trillion (10^{14})
Greece	Greek drachma	October 1944	13,800%	17.84%	4.3 days	100 Billion (10^{11})

(From: https://en.wikipedia.org/wiki/Hyperinflation)

When prices double in a matter of hours or days, it leads to massive instability, as people stop being willing to accept the money in exchange for goods and services because it loses value so quickly. For this reason, governments are very careful to avoid inflation getting too high.

Calculating Future Value

Calculations of future value must be adjusted for inflation.

- The interest rate stated by financial institutions will always be the nominal interest rate.
- Often when you have a nominal interest rate, you want to calculate the future value of a **real** cash flow.

Simple Example: You have $5000 in a savings account with nominal interest rate of 5%; what is the real value of your savings after one year if inflation is 2.4%?

- The nominal value of your savings after one year is $5000 \cdot 1.05 = 5250$. However, to get the real value of $5250, we must divide by one plus the inflation rate, so the real value is $\frac{5250}{1.024} = 5127$

14. You take out a loan for $10,000 with a nominal interest rate of 8.9%; inflation is 0.9%. How much will you owe, in real terms, after one year?

Generally speaking, for nominal interest rate r, and inflation rate i, the future value of a sum of money will be equal to the present value multiplied by the interest rate, then divided by the inflation rate.

- That is $FV = PV\left(\frac{1+r}{1+i}\right)$
- Two calculate the future value after another year, we repeat the process, so $FV = PV\left(\frac{1+r}{1+i}\right)^2$
- This means that after n years, $FV = PV\left(\frac{1+r}{1+i}\right)^n$

15. Consider your loan from the question above, what will be the value of your debt in real terms after 5 years? Assume the interest and inflation do not change and you do not make any payments.

Cash flow example: Suppose you are investing a cash flow with initial payment of $3500 that is growing at a rate of 5%, the nominal interest rate is 8%, and inflation is 0.7%. What is the value, in real terms, of your investment after 20 years of investing?

- We can look at the individual payments in a table, the same as we did previously for growing cash flows, only this time we must adjust for inflation.
- This gives us something like this:

Payment no.	Payment (EOP)	Inflation Adjusted Payment	Nominal Rate FV Factor	Real Rate FV Factor	Inflation Adjusted FV
1	$ 3,500.00	$ 3,475.67	3.95	3.46	$ 12,029.28
2	$ 3,675.00	$ 3,624.09	3.68	3.24	$ 11,749.52
3	$ 3,858.75	$ 3,778.84	3.42	3.04	$ 11,476.28
4	$ 4,051.69	$ 3,940.20	3.18	2.84	$ 11,209.39
5	$ 4,254.27	$ 4,108.45	2.96	2.66	$ 10,948.71
6	$ 4,466.99	$ 4,283.88	2.75	2.50	$ 10,694.08
7	$ 4,690.33	$ 4,466.81	2.56	2.34	$ 10,445.39
8	$ 4,924.85	$ 4,657.55	2.38	2.19	$ 10,202.47
9	$ 5,171.09	$ 4,856.43	2.22	2.05	$ 9,965.20
10	$ 5,429.65	$ 5,063.81	2.06	1.92	$ 9,733.45

Spreadsheet Connection

These tables are most easily created in a spreadsheet. Complete 'Unit 3 Topic 7 Inflation' to learn how to do this.

It is also possible to calculate real future value using the **growing payment formula**.

Example: Suppose you are investing a cash flow with initial payment of $800 that is growing at a rate of 2%, the nominal interest rate is 7%, and inflation is 1.2%. What is the value, in real terms, of your investment after 15 years of investing?

- The easiest way to do this is by first calculating the *Present Value* of the investment using the **growing payment formula**: $PV = \frac{c}{r-g}\left[1 - \frac{(1+g)^n}{(1+r)^n}\right] = \frac{800}{0.07-0.02}\left[1 - \frac{(1.02)^{15}}{(1.07)^{15}}\right] = 8195$
- To get the value after N years, we use the future value formula, discounting by inflation to give in term of today's dollars. So $FV = PV\left(\frac{1.07}{1.012}\right)^{15} = 18,900$

General Cash Flow: More generally, suppose you are investing a cash flow that is growing at rate g, you are earning interest at rate r, and inflation is i. What is the value, in current dollars, of your investment after n years of investing?

- We can calculate this by first calculating the *Present Value* of the investment using the growing payment formula: $PV = \frac{c}{r-g}[1 - \frac{(1+g)^n}{(1+r)^n}]$

- To get the value after n years, we use the future value formula, discounting by inflation to give in term of today's dollars. So $FV = PV(\frac{1+r}{1+i})^n$

- Putting the stages together, we get that $FV = \frac{c}{r-g}[1 - \frac{(1+g)^n}{(1+r)^n}](\frac{1+r}{1+i})^n$

Future Value with Inflation: $FV = \frac{c}{r-g}[1 - \frac{(1+g)^n}{(1+r)^n}](\frac{1+r}{1+i})^n$

Formula Key:

FV is the **future value** of the cash flow

r is the **interest rate**

g is the **growth rate**

i is the **inflation rate**

c is the **payment amount**

n is the **number of payments**

---

16. You make annual investments that earn interest at a rate of 5.3% with an initial payment of $2900 and growth rate of 2.5%. If inflation is 1.8%, what will the real value of your investments be after 8 years?

17. You make annual deposits in a savings account that earn interest at a rate of 1.1% with an initial payment of $11,000 and growth rate of 3%. If inflation is 2.1%, what will the real value of your investments be after 10 years?

200

Unit 3 Topic 7 Check for Understanding

Section 1

[Word Bank: deductions, hikes, nominal, real, positive, bribes, negative, match, steal, Social Security, decreases, increases]

1. When inflation goes up, the value of a dollar _____.
2. Interest rate that is not adjusted for inflation is known as _____ interest rate.
3. If a loaf of bread costs $3.50 at the being of the year and costs $3.10 at the end of the year, there has likely been _____ inflation.

Section 2

4. If you leave $1000 under your bed for five years, over which time inflation is at 1.2%, what will be the real value of your cash?

5. You put $2350 in a CD account with interest rate 1.8%. If inflation is 0.7%, how much will you have in the account after 3 years, in real terms?

6. Ruth is saving for her daughter's college fees. She will save for 10 years, with an initial deposit of $3200, a growth rate of 1.9%, and an interest rate of 4.2%. If inflation is 1.3%, how much will she have saved after 10 years?

7. Darryl Duck doesn't trust banks and so saves for retirement in cash – the first year he put $10,000 in cash in a safe in his basement, and he increases the amount by 1% each year. If inflation is constant at 2%, what will the value be of his savings when he retires after 20 years? (*Hint*: To use the **Future Value with Inflation** formula, note that in this example $r = 0$)

Unit Summary

This unit explains how to work with regular payments.
- Many loans and investments take the form of payments made or received at regular intervals.
- Calculating the present and future value of these cash flows requires working with geometric series.

The most important examples of regular payments are:
- Saving for retirement
- Paying off a mortgage
- Receiving dividends from investments

Here are the key equations for regular payments:

Recursive Formula for Arithmetic Sequences:
$$a_{n+1} = a_n + d$$

Explicit Formula for Geometric Sequence:
$$a_n = a_1 * R^{n-1}$$

Arithmetic Series Formula:
$$\sum_{t=1}^{n} a + (t-1) \cdot d = \left(a_1 + \frac{d(n-1)}{2}\right) \cdot n$$

Geometric Series Formula:
$$\sum_{i=0}^{n} a \cdot R^i = a\left(\frac{1 - R^{n+1}}{1 - R}\right)$$

Formula Key:

d is the **common difference**

R is the **common ratio** between the terms

a is the **initial constant**

a_n is the **nth term** of the sequence

a_1 is the **first term** of the sequence

n is the **number of terms** in the series

t is the **series variable**

Annuity Future Value:

$$FV = k\left(\frac{1 - (1 + r)^n}{-r}\right)$$

Annuity Present Value:

$$PV = \frac{c}{r}\left(1 - \frac{1}{(1 + r)^n}\right)$$

Formula Key:

PV is the **present value** of the annuity

r is the **interest rate**

c is the **payment amount**

n is the **number of payments** in the annuity

Growing Payment Formula:

$$PV = \frac{c}{r - g}\left[1 - \frac{(1 + g)^n}{(1 + r)^n}\right]$$

Perpetuity Formula:

$$PV = \frac{c}{r}$$

Dividend Discount Formula:

$$PV = \frac{c}{r - g}$$

Future Value with Inflation:

$$FV = \frac{c}{r - g}\left[1 - \frac{(1 + g)^n}{(1 + r)^n}\right]\left(\frac{1 + r}{1 + i}\right)^n$$

Formula Key:

PV is the **present value**

FV is the **future value**

r is the **discounting rate**

g is the **growth rate**

c is the **payment amount**

n is the **number of payments**

i is the **inflation rate**

GLOSSARY

Annuity: A form of investment in which you receive periodic (generally monthly or annual) payments.

Arithmetic Sequence: a sequence of numbers which increases by a constant amount

Arithmetic Series: the sum of an arithmetic sequence

Common Difference: the constant amount by which the terms increase

Common Ratio: the constant amount by which the terms are multiplied

Constant payments: When the amount paid or received from an investment is the same each month.

Debt to income ratio: The ratio between required payment on a loan (debt) and a person's income – used to decide whether person is eligible for a loan.

Discounting: Calculating how much a given amount paid in the future is worth now.

Discounting equation: $PV = FV(1 + r)^{-t}$

Dividend: Payment shareholders receive coming from a company's profits.

Dividend discount formula: $PV = \dfrac{c}{r-g}$

Down payment: The initial payment a person must make when buying a house in order to be granted a mortgage. This amount becomes the person's "equity" in the home.

Explicit Formula: allows you to calculate the value of a term in a sequence as a function of its index without making reference to previous terms in the sequence

Future Value Factor: tells you how much one dollar at the time of payment is worth at the term of the annuity. Equation: $(1 + r)^{n+1-i}$

Geometric Sequence: a sequence of numbers where each term is equal to the previous one multiplied by a constant

Geometric Series: the sum of a geometric sequence

Growing Payments: When the amount paid or received from an investment increases each month.

Growth Factor: how much bigger, proportionally, a payment is than the original payment

Index/term number: the place a term occurs in the sequence

Inflation: Increase in the cost in dollars to buy items over time, often measured by the consumer price index (CPI) which is the cost to buy a "basket" of goods and services.

Initial Constant: the first term in a sequence

Interest: This may be fixed or adjustable.
- A **fixed-rate mortgage** has a constant interest rate over the term of the loan.
- An **adjustable-rate mortgage** has an interest rate that may move up or down over the term of the loan.

Investment: Transferring present wealth to the future to allow for future consumption.

Loan to Value Ratio: what proportion of the value of the house the loan will cover

Mortgage: A loan used to buy or finance a house, where the house is collateral for the loan.

Payments: This is how much must be paid back towards the debt each period.

Perpetuity: a sequence of constant payments that doesn't stop

Present Value Factor: current value of a dollar received at some point in the future

Principal: The initial investment amount

Recursive Definition: a definition of a sequence that tells you how to get the next term by performing an operation on the previous term

Retirement: the period in which people have stopped working

Sigma Notation: 'Σ' means sum: when you have $\sum_{t=1}^{n}$ followed by a formula containing t, you take the sequence obtained by substituting numbers 1 to n for t, and add them together.

Term: how long it takes to completely pay off the loan